THE SLOW COOKER
solution

THE SLOW COOKER
solution

GO SLOW AND
EAT WELL

NOURISHING RECIPES
PACKED WITH FLAVOUR

LOVE FOOD™

This edition published by Parragon Books Ltd in 2015
LOVE FOOD is an imprint of Parragon Books Ltd

Parragon Books Ltd
Chartist House
15–17 Trim Street
Bath BA1 1HA, UK
www.parragon.com/lovefood

ISBN 978-1-4748-0463-9

Printed in China

New recipes by Georgina Fuggle
New photography, including cover photography,
by Mike Cooper
Home economy for new photography by
Lincoln Jefferson

NOTES FOR THE READER

This book uses both metric and imperial measurements.
Follow the same units of measurement throughout; do
not mix metric and imperial. All spoon measurements
are level: teaspoons are assumed to be 5 ml, and
tablespoons are assumed to be 15 ml. Unless otherwise
stated, milk is assumed to be full fat, eggs and individual
vegetables are medium, pepper is freshly ground black
pepper and salt is table salt.
Unless otherwise stated, all root vegetables should be
peeled prior to using.

The times given are an approximate guide only.
Preparation times differ according to the techniques
used by different people and the cooking times may also
vary from those given.

Please note that any ingredients stated as being optional,
are not included in the nutritional values provided. The
nutritional values given are approximate and provided
as a guideline only, they do not account for individual
cooks, scales and portion sizes. The nutritional values
provided are per serving.

For best results, use a food thermometer when
cooking meat. Check the latest government guidelines
for current advice.

Agency images courtesy of Shutterstock and iStock.

Contents

INTRODUCTION

Slow cooking has been a revered cooking technique since ancient times. It is, quite simply, the best way to produce healthy vegetable dishes with deep flavour and meat so tender it falls from the bone. But with our busy modern lives, slow cookers are a welcome convenience for anyone who is out of the house all day, and who wants to return to a delicious, ready-to-eat, home-cooked meal.

Since its invention in the 1970s, the slow cooker has gained a reputation as a great set-it-and-forget-it gadget for producing finished meals with minimal effort. The slow cooker doesn't provide convenience at the expense of quality or flavour. In fact, it can produce dishes – ranging from starters to desserts – that are full of nutrients and taste fantastic. As meat, stock, vegetables and herbs simmer together their flavours emerge, intensify and marry into a whole far more enticing than the ingredients might suggest.

The slow cooker is ideal for making flavour-packed stocks and soups, turning economical cuts of meat into rich stews, and transforming dried beans and root vegetables into wholesome meals. It is also great for cooking more delicate meats, fish and vegetables, because the ingredients are cooked gently without being broken down. More surprisingly the slow cooker can be used to cook cakes and other desserts – this comes in handy when you don't want to heat up your kitchen during hot weather or if you are using your oven for a turkey or a roast.

Because the slow cooker uses very little electricity (less than a light bulb!), it is both safe and economical to turn it on in the morning and leave it unattended all day. And because the temperature is low and constant, the majority of dishes won't overcook, even after being left for 8 hours or more.

Just think about it for a moment – what could be better than to arrive home after a long day to be greeted by the enticing aroma of a ready-to-eat home-cooked meal?

CHOOSING THE RIGHT SLOW COOKER

There are a vast array of slow cookers – from tiny models to giant pots, each coming with or without a myriad of options and special features. Take time to determine which slow cooker is right for you. They vary widely in price, from the most basic and inexpensive models to high-tech computerized machines. The good news is that it is possible to find a good-quality slow cooker in any price range. Small models with only the most basic settings are surprisingly affordable.

SIZE AND SHAPE

A 3.8-litre/6½-pint slow cooker is ideal for a family of four or five, while a 1.9-litre/3¼-pint cooker might be perfect for a couple. Larger cookers are great for large families, people who entertain or those who like to cook a big dish and freeze leftovers. Many recipes here can be prepared in a 1.9-litre/3¼-pint slow cooker, but some slow cookers may need liquid volumes adjusted where ingredients need to be covered.

For most dishes – soups, stews and the like – the shape of the slow cooker is irrelevant, but some dishes are better suited to a particular shape. Oval slow cookers can easily fit big roasts, turkey breasts, leg shanks and other large cuts of meat. If you plan to make a lot of cakes, a round slow cooker is a better bet. Models vary from one manufacturer to another, so check the instructions, although the basics will apply to all models.

PROGRAMMABILITY

The most basic slow cooker models offer three settings: high, low and off. These models are inexpensive and work just fine, but for models with no built-in timer you'll need a separate timer so you can programme the correct cooking time.

More expensive models often offer programming features that range from multiple time/temperature settings (such as 'high 4 hours' or 'low 8 hours') to an automatic switch-to-warm feature. Other models allow you to set your own parameters for temperature and timing down to the minute. The more control you have over the settings, the more flexibility you have – and the more you'll pay for the privilege.

If you plan to use your slow cooker mostly when you will be around the house, a basic model may suit you. If, on the other hand, you hope to set your cooker in the morning before heading off to work for the day, consider one that includes a built-in timer and will automatically switch to 'warm' when the time is up.

7

VERSATILITY

Most slow cookers come with a ceramic cooking vessel that is too porous for use on the hob. There are, however, a few high-end models with cooking inserts that can go from hob to slow cooker and back again. You'll pay for this luxury, but you'll save time and energy, by not having to transfer ingredients from one pot to another, and reduce the number of dishes you need to wash. Some slow cookers are portable and come fitted with hinged locking lids, carrying handles and specially designed carrying cases and straps to help you transport food easily.

A few of the recipes in this book need a metal trivet. This is sometimes useful when you are baking bread or cakes, or when roasting a chicken so that the chicken doesn't sit on the base of the slow cooker and become scorched. Some slow cookers come with a trivet. If yours doesn't, then you can use aluminium foil shaped into balls or into a ring to support the ingredient. Other options for slow cooker trivets are a metal canning ring or a large onion cut into big chunks to support the baking container or ingredient.

CLEANING, MAINTENANCE AND SAFETY

Do follow the manufacturer's guidelines for cleaning and maintaining your slow cooker.

While the glass lid of many models is dishwasher safe, the ceramic cooking vessel that comes with most models is not. This is because the ceramic material is porous, which is what makes it retain heat. Submerging it in water for long periods will cause it to absorb water, and affect its ability to retain heat. Unless your slow cooker's manual says that it is dishwasher safe, wash it by hand and never leave it submerged in water for a long period. If you encounter stuck-on food, fill it with warm soapy water and leave it to soak for a little before scrubbing it out.

Be careful never to plunge the hot ceramic pot into cold water as this sudden temperature change may cause it to crack. Instead, fill it with warm water or, better still, allow the pot to cool before cleaning it. The electric base should never be submerged in water. To clean it, unplug it and then use a damp sponge or cloth to wipe off any food that may have dripped onto the outside of the slow cooker.

TIPS FOR SUCCESS

The outer casing and lid may become very hot during cooking, so place the cooker so that it is not too close to walls, curtains, cords or other flammable items when it is in use. Use oven gloves when touching any part of the slow cooker after it has been on for any period of time.

Always keep refrigerated foods cold until you are ready to add them to the slow cooker. If using frozen meat, poultry, fish or shellfish, it is best to thaw it thoroughly before adding to the slow cooker. If you choose to add it while it is still frozen, you may need to adjust the final cooking time to ensure that the meat is thoroughly cooked.

The slow cooker allows you to 'set-it-and-forget-it', but many foods benefit from a little preparation. Browning meat, for example, contributes to the overall flavour of a dish and seals in the meat's juices, keeping it from drying out during cooking.

Don't stint on the slow cooking times. The longer and slower your food cooks, the more time it has to develop the depth of flavour that makes it delicious.

Because slow cooker lids are designed to be more or less airtight, sauces and stocks won't reduce the way they do on the hob. Because of this, adding too much liquid to your slow cooker can render meat dry, vegetables flavourless and sauces bland. Since the slow cooker retains all of the ingredients' natural moisture, a minimal amount of added liquid is sufficient for most dishes. If, however, you are cooking a dish where you'd like to have a thick sauce, try setting the lid of the slow cooker ajar for the last hour or so of cooking – this allows steam to escape and the liquid to reduce. Avoid doing this too early, or you'll lose too much of the heat and there is a danger that your food may not cook properly.

COOK IT SLOW

After a quick guide to the classic ingredients used in slow cooking, the recipes that follow are designed to be easy to use – with short ingredients lists and minimal steps – but they never skimp on flavour. Whether your goal is to offer simple, nutritious weekday meals for your family or to impress your guests with a meal that seems to have taken more effort to prepare than it did, you'll find all the inspiration and recipes you need right here. Happy slow cooking!

CLASSIC INGREDIENTS FOR SLOW COOKING

The ingredients suitable for slow cooking can be wide-ranging — as the following pages show — but there are likely to be some stalwarts that will feature large in the dishes you choose to cook.

POULTRY

The dark meat portions of poultry – drumsticks, thighs and wings – suit slow cooking. Chicken breasts are also delicious when they are browned first in a frying pan. If your slow cooker is large enough, you can also cook a whole bird.

PASTA, RICE AND WHOLEGRAINS

One of the benefits of slow cookers is that most of the ingredients, sometimes all of them, can be added at the beginning, leaving you free to do other things. Wholegrains such as pearl barley or bulgar can often be added to the slow cooker early in the process. In other cases, ingredients such as pasta and rice will either need to be added towards the end or prepared separately, to serve with the slow-cooked dish.

SAUTÉED VEGETABLES

Onions and garlic contribute significantly to the flavour of slow-cooked dishes and sautéing them before adding them to the slow cooker deepens their flavour and the taste of the final dish.

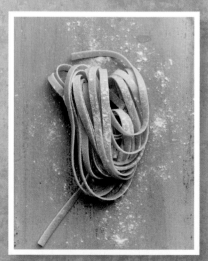

BEANS

Beans are perfect for long, slow cooking. Bean stews and vegetarian chillies – like those made with meat – become thick, rich and deeply flavoured after several hours in the slow cooker. It is important to pre-soak and cook beans prior to adding them to the slow cooker – see the food safety note below.

ROOT VEGETABLES

Hardy vegetables, such as potatoes, onions, carrots, turnips, winter squashes and fennel turn deeply flavoured and tender after long, slow braising. They won't disintegrate but will be fork-tender and rich with the other flavours, herbs and spices you include.

MEAT

Fattier cuts of meat, such as chuck, shoulder, shank and rump, are ideally suited to low-and-slow cooking. Less expensive than leaner cuts, you can also use less of these fattier cuts because slow-cooking extracts a meaty flavour that permeates the whole dish. You can trim off the fat before putting them in the slow cooker to give you a healthier result. Browning meat before adding it to the slow cooker also renders a good deal of the fat, so it is recommended for some cuts of meat. The resulting caramelized crust also contributes to the overall flavour of the dish.

SPICES

Adding spices to the sautéed onions and garlic and allowing them to cook for a moment or two will also help the flavours of the finished dish to marry.

FOOD SAFETY NOTE

Dried beans cooked in the slow cooker have been linked to food poisoning. To be safe, soak dried beans for at least 5 hours prior to cooking, and then drain and rinse them, place them in a saucepan, cover with cold water, bring to the boil over a medium–high heat and cook at a rapid boil for at least 10 minutes. Remove from the heat, rinse and drain one more time, and then place the beans in the slow cooker, cover with at least 2.5 cm/1 inch of cold water and cook on low, covered, for about 8–10 hours, until tender. To prevent the beans becoming tough, do not add salt until after cooking.

Chapter 1

NOURISH

Your slow cooker can provide the food to support growth and development and keep you and your family in the best of health.

KALE, QUINOA AND CAULIFLOWER SOUP

This healthy soup is packed with nutrients and the quinoa gives it extra substance. Serve with crusty bread for a warming lunch.

SERVES: 4   PREP: 20 MINUTES   COOK: 4 HOURS 10 MINUTES

2 tbsp olive oil

2 small onions, finely diced

4 garlic cloves, sliced

1 tsp smoked paprika, plus a pinch for garnish

100 g/3½ oz quinoa

2 litres/3½ pints hot vegetable stock or chicken stock

1 small head cauliflower, about 250 g/9 oz, broken into very small florets

200 g/7 oz curly kale, washed and finely chopped

zest and juice of 1 lemon

100 g/3½ oz chorizo, sliced

salt and pepper (optional)

2 tbsp roughly chopped fresh flat-leaf parsley, to garnish

4 tbsp natural yogurt, to serve

1. Heat the olive oil in a large frying pan. Add the onion and garlic and cook over a medium heat for 3–4 minutes until soft. Sprinkle over the smoked paprika and cook for a further minute.

2. Add the onion and garlic to the slow cooker with the quinoa, stock and cauliflower. Cover and cook on high for 3 hours.

3. Stir in the kale, re-cover and cook for a further hour. Season with salt and pepper, if using, and stir through the lemon zest and juice.

4. While the soup is cooking, heat a small frying pan over a medium heat. Add the chorizo and fry until crispy.

5. Ladle the soup into bowls, add the chorizo, garnish with parsley and paprika and add a tablespoon of yogurt to each bowl.

14

Per serving: 353 kcals | 20.7g fat | 6.1g sat fat | 32g carbs | 5.6g sugar | 6g fibre | 14.5g protein | 3.3g salt

PEPPERS STUFFED WITH FARRO, FETA AND HERBS

Slow cooking the peppers produces a lovely, tender flesh, which sits beautifully with the nutty farro and tangy feta cheese.

SERVES 4   PREP: 20 MINUTES   COOK: 3–4 HOURS

4 large peppers
200 g/7 oz farro, cooked
2 garlic cloves, crushed
100 g/3½ oz black olives, stoned and halved
5 spring onions, finely sliced
100 g/3½ oz feta cheese, crumbled
2 tbsp chopped fresh basil
2 tbsp chopped fresh parsley
2 tbsp olive oil
salt and pepper (optional)

1. Slice the tops off the peppers just below the stems, remove the seeds and slice a very thin layer from the base of each one so they will sit flat in the slow cooker.

2. Put the farro, garlic, olives, spring onions, feta, herbs and oil in a large mixing bowl and combine well. Season with salt and pepper, if using.

3. Using a large spoon, stuff the mixture into the peppers, add the pepper tops and then place them in the base of the slow cooker. Cover and cook on high for 3–4 hours, until the peppers are tender. Serve immediately.

16

Top Tip

USE ROBUST PEPPERS THAT ARE ABLE TO WITHSTAND SLOW COOKING – IF THEY ARE TOO SMALL THEY HAVE A TENDENCY TO COLLAPSE.

Per serving: 295 kcals | 15.8g fat | 5.1g sat fat | 30.2g carbs | 8.5g sugar | 6.4g fibre | 8.3g protein | 1g salt

BLACK BEAN CHILLI WITH SMOKED CHIPOTLE AND RED PEPPER

This delicious, lightly smoked chilli combines black beans and chipotle. Full of goodness, this is ideal comfort food.

SERVES 4   PREP: 25 MINUTES   COOK: 8 HOURS

250 g/9 oz dried black beans, soaked overnight, or for at least 5 hours
500 ml/17 fl oz boiling water
1 dried chipotle chilli
2 onions, sliced
3 garlic cloves, sliced
1 tsp ground cumin
1 tsp smoked paprika
500 g/1 lb 2 oz passata
1 tbsp tomato purée
3 red peppers, deseeded and sliced
1 large courgette, sliced
1 avocado, sliced, to garnish
2 tbsp chopped fresh coriander, to garnish
4 tbsp sour cream, to serve

1. Drain and rinse the beans, place in a saucepan, cover with fresh cold water, and bring to the boil. Boil rapidly for at least 10 minutes, then remove from the heat, drain and rinse again.

2. Pour the boiling water over the chipotle chilli and allow it to soak for 5 minutes. Remove the chilli from the water, keeping the liquid to one side, and finely slice the chilli.

3. Put the chilli, onions, garlic, cumin, paprika, beans, passata, tomato purée, peppers and courgette into the slow cooker. Add the chipotle water, cover the slow cooker and cook on low for 8 hours.

4. Transfer to warmed plates, garnish each one with avocado and coriander and serve with a tablespoon of sour cream on each serving.

19

Top Tip

THE SMOKY TASTE OF THE CHIPOTLE CHILLI IS KEY TO THIS DISH, BUT IF IT IS HARD TO LOCATE, DOUBLE THE AMOUNT OF SMOKED PAPRIKA.

Per serving: 422 kcals | 11.6g fat | 2.7g sat fat | 63.3g carbs | 15.6g sugar | 18.4g fibre | 19.6g protein | 0.2g salt

CAVOLO NERO, GOAT'S CHEESE AND SUN-DRIED TOMATO FRITTATA

Slow cooker frittatas are light, moist and flavourful.
The goat's cheese could be replaced with mozzarella or feta.

SERVES 4   PREP: 15 MINUTES   COOK: 3 HOURS 10 MINUTES

1 tbsp olive oil, plus extra to brush the slow cooker

1 medium onion, roughly chopped

3 garlic cloves, roughly chopped

200 g/7 oz cavolo nero, shredded

8 eggs, beaten

8 sun-dried tomatoes, drained and roughly chopped

2 tbsp roughly chopped fresh parsley

100 g/3½ oz goat's cheese, crumbled

salt and pepper (optional)

1. Heat the oil in a large frying pan over a medium heat. Add the onion and cook over a low heat, stirring occasionally, for 3–4 minutes until softened. Add the garlic and cavolo nero and leave for a further 5 minutes.

2. Meanwhile stir the eggs, sun-dried tomatoes, parsley and half the goat's cheese through the onion mixture. Season well with salt and pepper, if using.

3. Lightly brush the inside of your slow cooker with oil and pour in the frittata mixture. Crumble the remaining goat's cheese over the surface.

4. Cover the slow cooker and cook on low for 2½–3 hours, or until the frittata is set and beginning to brown at the edges. Serve warm, or leave to cool.

21

Top Tip

THE FRITTATA CAN BE EATEN WARM OR COLD, AND IT'S A DELICIOUS COMPONENT OF A SUMMER PICNIC.

Per serving: 329 kcals | 22.9g fat | 9g sat fat | 10.8g carbs | 4.2g sugar | 2.9g fibre | 21.2g protein | 0.7g salt

KOREAN BEEF STEW WITH KIMCHI AND SESAME

Kimchi, a staple of Korean cuisine, marries raw vegetables and spices. Here it adds significant depth of flavour to the stew.

SERVES 4   PREP: 15 MINUTES   COOK: 8 HOURS

900 g/2 lb chuck steak
500 g/1 lb 2 oz kimchi
1 large onion, sliced
1 tbsp grated fresh ginger
4 garlic cloves, crushed
1 bay leaf
¼ tsp pepper
2 tbsp rice wine
2 tbsp sesame oil
1 tbsp soy sauce
¼ tsp chilli powder
200 ml/7 fl oz water
salt (optional)
4 spring onions, chopped, to garnish
1 tbsp sesame seeds, to garnish
700 g/1 lb 9 oz freshly cooked black rice, to serve

1. Remove any obvious fat from the steak and cut it into 2–3-cm/¾–1¼-inch cubes. Place the steak, kimchi, onion, ginger, garlic, bay leaf, pepper, rice wine, oil, soy sauce and chilli powder in the slow cooker. Pour the water over and mix gently until combined. Season with salt, if using.

2. Cover the slow cooker and cook on low for 8 hours, stirring every couple of hours, if you can. Remove the bay leaf, transfer to warmed serving bowls, garnish with spring onions and sesame seeds and serve with black rice.

22

Top Tip

THE STEW WILL BE COOKED AFTER SIX HOURS, BUT THE EXTRA TIME MEANS THAT THE MEAT WILL BECOME ALL THE MORE TENDER.

Per serving: 667 kcals | 26.4g fat | 8.8g sat fat | 48.9g carbs | 2.1g sugar | 6.9g fibre | 57g protein | 2.2g salt

BAKED AUBERGINE WITH COURGETTE

A Mediterranean-inspired dish that combines the familiar vegetable mix of ratatouille in a crumb-topped bake.

SERVES 4   PREP: 20–25 MINUTES   COOK: 4 HOURS 10 MINUTES

2 large aubergines
1 tbsp olive oil, for brushing
2 large courgettes, sliced
4 tomatoes, sliced
1 garlic clove, finely chopped
15 g/½ oz dry breadcrumbs
15 g/½ oz freshly grated
Parmesan cheese
salt and pepper (optional)
16 basil leaves, to garnish

1. Cut the aubergines into fairly thin slices and brush with oil. Heat a large griddle pan or heavy-based frying pan over a high heat, then add the aubergines and cook in batches for 6–8 minutes, turning once, until soft and brown.

2. Layer the aubergines in the slow cooker with the courgettes, tomatoes and garlic, seasoning with salt and pepper, if using, between the layers.

3. Mix the breadcrumbs with the cheese and sprinkle over the vegetables. Cover and cook on low for 4 hours.

4. Transfer to warmed serving bowls, garnish with basil leaves and serve immediately.

24

Top Tip

USE AUBERGINES WITH A SMOOTH, SHINY SKIN – AVOID WRINKLES OR DULL SKIN, WHICH MEANS THE AUBERGINE IS PAST ITS BEST.

Per serving: 169 kcals | 5.6g fat | 1.3g sat fat | 27.1g carbs | 15.6g sugar | 10.9g fibre | 6.9g protein | 0.2g salt

WINTER VEGETABLE MEDLEY

Serve this herb-flavoured vegetable stew with brown rice or pasta for a tasty and nutritious meal.

SERVES 4   PREP: 15–20 MINUTES   COOK: 3¼ HOURS

2 tbsp sunflower oil
2 onions, chopped
3 carrots, chopped
3 parsnips, chopped
2 heads of celery, chopped
2 tbsp chopped fresh parsley
1 tbsp chopped fresh coriander
300 ml/10 fl oz vegetable stock
salt and pepper (optional)

1. Heat the oil in a large, heavy-based saucepan. Add the onions and cook over a medium heat, stirring occasionally, for 5 minutes until softened. Add the carrots, parsnips and celery and cook, stirring occasionally, for a further 5 minutes. Stir in the herbs, season with salt and pepper, if using, and pour in the stock. Bring to the boil.

2. Transfer the vegetable mixture to the slow cooker, cover and cook on high for 3 hours until tender. Taste and adjust the seasoning if necessary. Using a slotted spoon, transfer the vegetables to warmed plates, then spoon over a little of the cooking liquid. Serve immediately.

27

Top Tip

SERVE THE VEGETABLE MEDLEY WITH TOASTED SEEDS OR NUTS ON TOP TO ADD A COMPLEMENTARY CRUNCH.

Per serving: 202 kcals | 8.1g fat | 1g sat fat | 31g carbs | 11.6g sugar | 10g fibre | 3.8g protein | 1.3g salt

SLOW-COOKED GOODNESS

A nourishing meal gives sustenance, supports growth and keeps us in the best of health. It can also make us feel good, give us energy and stabilize our mood. It's good to know, then, that the staples of slow cooking – from fresh and colourful vegetables to wholegrains, meat and chicken – are bursting with nutrients. So if you are using a slow cooker to prepare your meals, they are likely to have a high nutrient content.

VEGETABLES

Along with fruit, vegetables are the mainstay of a healthy diet. We are advised to eat at least five portions a day, and a slow cooker makes this task much easier. Root vegetables – such as carrots, swedes, turnips, potatoes and parsnips – are classic choices for slow cooking. Because they are dense, they take longer to cook, in the process absorbing multiple flavours from the other ingredients.

Other vegetables – ranging from spring greens, kale and celery to artichoke, broccoli and cauliflower – are also slow cooker favourites. These vegetables are full of fibre, Vitamins K, A, C and iron and calcium, and being less dense are generally added towards the end of the cooking time. It is also true that naturally sweet vegetables – such as sweetcorn, carrots and sweet potatoes – add a healthy sweetness to slow cooker meals, which can reduce the yearning for less-healthy sweet treats.

WHOLEGRAINS

Eating wholegrains such as brown rice, pearl barley, bulgar and quinoa gives you long-lasting energy and, combined with a balanced diet, they lower the risk of chronic diseases. Wholegrains can easily be added to the slow cooker – there just needs to be enough liquid for the grain to absorb. Many slow cooker recipes can also be served with couscous or quinoa, brown rice or wild rice, which are easy to prepare as your slow cooked meal reaches its final stages.

BEANS

From cannellini beans and black beans to kidney beans and black-eyed peas, beans are a rich source of calcium and are also high in fibre and protein and low in fat, sugar and sodium. It is important to soak beans before cooking, draining, rinsing and boiling them for about 10 minutes – they will then become deeply flavoured after several hours cooking. Beans are also absorbed slowly, so are good for controlling blood sugar or for helping with weight loss.

MEAT

A nutritious meat stew is a classic slow-cooked dish. All meat offers protein, fat, iron, selenium, zinc and B vitamins. It's the tougher (and cheaper) cuts of meat such as brisket, shoulder of lamb or chicken thigh pieces that are ideal for slow cooking. This is because the process breaks down the tissue until the meat becomes melting and tender – and packed with flavour.

WHITE BEAN STEW

This rich and healthy stew with white cannellini beans and an array of vegetables has an impressive flavour.

SERVES 4   PREP: 25 MINUTES   COOK: 3 HOURS 20 MINUTES – 6 HOURS 20 MINUTES

2 tbsp olive oil
1 onion, diced
2 garlic cloves, finely chopped
2 carrots, diced
2 celery sticks, diced
175 g/6 oz canned tomato purée
1 tsp salt
½ tsp pepper
¼ – ½ tsp crushed dried red pepper flakes
1 bay leaf
225 ml/8 fl oz dry white wine
850 g/1 lb 14 oz canned cannellini beans, rinsed and drained
250 g/9 oz chard, kale or other winter green, stems and thick centre ribs removed, leaves cut into wide ribbons
225 ml/8 fl oz water
25 g/1 oz freshly grated Parmesan cheese, to serve

1. Heat the oil in a large frying pan over a medium–high heat. Add the onion and garlic and cook, stirring, for about 5 minutes, until soft. Add the carrots and celery and cook for a further few minutes. Stir in the tomato purée, salt, pepper, red pepper flakes and bay leaf, then add the wine.

2. Bring to the boil and cook, stirring and scraping up any sediment from the base of the pan, for about 5 minutes, until most of the liquid has evaporated. Transfer the mixture to the slow cooker.

3. Stir in the beans, chard and water. Cover and cook on high for 3 hours or on low for 6 hours. Remove the bay leaf and serve hot, garnished with the cheese.

30

Per serving: 443 kcals | 10.1g fat | 2.2g sat fat | 51.7g carbs | 10.5g sugar | 19.5g fibre | 21.7g protein | 2.2g salt

GINGER-STEAMED HALIBUT WITH TOMATOES AND BEANS

This light and healthy main dish has a fresh and attractive appearance and is full of delicate flavours.

SERVES 4   PREP: 25–30 MINUTES, PLUS MARINATING   COOK: 2 HOURS

1 tbsp finely chopped fresh ginger

2 garlic cloves, finely chopped

1–2 hot red chillies, deseeded and diced

2 tbsp Thai fish sauce

2 tbsp mirin or other sweet white wine

1 tsp sugar

4 halibut fillets (about 675 g/ 1 lb 8 oz in total)

1 tbsp vegetable oil, for oiling

350 g/12 oz French beans, topped and tailed

450 g/1 lb cherry tomatoes, halved, or quartered if large

To garnish

4 spring onions, thinly sliced

finely chopped fresh coriander

6 fresh basil leaves, shredded

1. Put the ginger, garlic, chillies, fish sauce, mirin and sugar into a baking dish large enough to hold the fish and stir to combine. Add the fish and turn to coat in the mixture. Cover and place in the refrigerator to marinate for 30 minutes.

2. Meanwhile, brush four large squares of baking paper with oil.

3. Divide the beans evenly between the prepared squares of paper, piling them in the middle. Scatter the tomatoes evenly over them. Top each pile of vegetables with a fish fillet and some of the marinade. Fold up the packets securely, leaving a little room for the steam to circulate, and place them in the slow cooker. Cover and cook on high for about 2 hours, until the halibut is flaky and cooked through.

4. To serve, carefully remove the packets from the slow cooker, open them and slide the contents onto warmed plates, then garnish with spring onions, coriander and basil.

33

Top Tip

DON'T LEAVE THE FISH IN THE SLOW COOKER TO KEEP IT WARM AFTER IT IS COOKED – THIS WILL DRY IT OUT.

Per serving: 272 kcals | 6.1g fat | 1.1g sat fat | 17.9g carbs | 10.8g sugar | 4.4g fibre | 35.1g protein | 2.3g salt

TOFU WITH SPICY PEANUT SAUCE

Nutritious tofu gets a powerful punch of flavour from a combination of peanut butter, garlic, chillies and coriander.

SERVES 4   PREP: 20 MINUTES   COOK: 4¼ HOURS

675 g/1 lb 8 oz extra-firm tofu
2 tbsp vegetable oil
85 g/3 oz smooth peanut butter
3 tbsp low-sodium soy sauce
3 tbsp unseasoned rice vinegar
juice of 1 lime
2 tbsp soft light brown sugar
2 tsp toasted sesame oil
2 garlic cloves, finely chopped
1 tbsp finely chopped fresh ginger
2 jalapeño chillies, deseeded and finely chopped
350 g/12 oz baby spinach leaves
1 tbsp chopped fresh coriander, to serve, and 1 tbsp chopped fresh coriander, to garnish
700 g/1lb 9 oz steamed rice, to serve

34

1. Slice the tofu into 2.5-cm/1-inch thick slabs and pat very dry with kitchen paper, pressing to release any excess moisture. Cut into 2.5-cm/1-inch cubes.

2. Heat the vegetable oil in a large, non-stick frying pan over a medium–high heat. Add the tofu, in batches, if necessary, and cook on one side for about 3 minutes, until brown. Turn and cook on the other side for a further 3 minutes, until brown.

3. Meanwhile, put the peanut butter, soy sauce, vinegar, lime juice, sugar, sesame oil, garlic, ginger and chillies into the slow cooker and mix to combine.

4. Add the tofu to the slow cooker. Stir gently to coat, cover and cook on low for about 4 hours.

5. About 15 minutes before serving, place the spinach in the slow cooker on top of the cooked tofu mixture, cover and cook for about 15 minutes, until the spinach is wilted. Stir in 1 tablespoon of the coriander and serve immediately, garnished with the remaining coriander, with steamed rice.

Top Tip

TOFU IS A CLASSY SLOW COOKER ACT, THOROUGHLY ABSORBING THE FLAVOURS OF THE OTHER INGREDIENTS.

Per serving: 669 kcals | 29.3g fat | 4.4g sat fat | 73.8g carbs | 11.4g sugar | 6.6g fibre | 30.5g protein | 1.4g salt

CHICKEN AND APPLE POT

In this recipe the soft, melting cooking apple adds sharpness while the caramelized eating apples give sweetness and crunch.

SERVES 4   PREP: 25 MINUTES   COOK: 7 HOURS 40 MINUTES

1 tbsp olive oil

4 chicken portions, about 175 g/6 oz each

1 onion, chopped

2 celery sticks, roughly chopped

1½ tbsp plain flour

300 ml/10 fl oz clear apple juice

150 ml/5 fl oz chicken stock

1 cooking apple, peeled, cored and cut into quarters

2 bay leaves

1–2 tsp clear honey

1 yellow pepper, deseeded and cut into chunks

salt and pepper (optional)

To garnish

1 large or 2 medium eating apples, cored and sliced

1 tbsp melted butter

2 tbsp demerara sugar

1 tbsp chopped fresh mint

1. Heat the oil in a heavy-based frying pan. Add the chicken and cook over a medium–high heat, turning frequently, for 10 minutes, until golden brown. Transfer to the slow cooker. Add the onion and celery to the pan and cook over a low heat for 5 minutes, until softened. Sprinkle in the flour and cook for 2 minutes, then remove the pan from the heat.

2. Gradually stir in the apple juice and stock, then return the pan to the heat and bring to the boil. Stir in the cooking apple, bay leaves and honey and season with salt and pepper, if using. Pour the mixture over the chicken in the slow cooker, cover and cook on low for 6½ hours, until the chicken is tender and cooked through. Stir in the yellow pepper, re-cover and cook on high for 45 minutes.

3. Shortly before serving, preheat the grill. Brush one side of the eating apple slices with half the melted butter and sprinkle with half the sugar. Cook under the preheated grill for 2–3 minutes, until the sugar has caramelized. Turn the slices over with tongs, brush with the remaining butter and sprinkle with the remaining sugar. Grill for a further 2 minutes. Remove the bay leaves, transfer the stew to warmed plates and garnish with the caramelized apple slices and the mint. Serve immediately.

37

Per serving: 409 kcals | 14.9g fat | 4.6g sat fat | 39.1g carbs | 30g sugar | 3.9g fibre | 27.2g protein | 0.6g salt

SOUTH-WESTERN SEAFOOD STEW

The flavours of lime and fresh coriander leaves give this healthy yet hearty fish stew a rich flavour.

SERVES 4   PREP: 25 MINS   COOK: 8¼ HOURS

3 tbsp olive oil

1 large onion, chopped

4 garlic cloves, finely chopped

1 yellow pepper, deseeded and chopped

1 red pepper, deseeded and chopped

1 orange pepper, deseeded and chopped

450 g/1 lb tomatoes, peeled and chopped

2 large mild green chillies, such as poblano, chopped

finely grated rind and juice of 1 lime

2 tbsp chopped fresh coriander, plus extra leaves to garnish

1 bay leaf

450 ml/15 fl oz fish, vegetable or chicken stock

450 g/1 lb red mullet fillets

450 g/1 lb raw prawns

225 g/8 oz prepared squid

salt and pepper (optional)

38

1. Heat 2 tbsp of the oil in a saucepan. Add the onion and garlic and cook over a low heat, stirring occasionally, for 5 minutes, until softened. Add the peppers, tomatoes and chillies and cook, stirring frequently, for 5 minutes. Stir in the lime rind and juice, add the chopped coriander and bay leaf and pour in the stock. Bring to the boil, stirring occasionally.

2. Transfer the mixture to the slow cooker, cover and cook on low for 7½ hours. Meanwhile, skin the fish fillets, if necessary, and cut the flesh into chunks. Peel and devein the prawns. Cut the squid bodies into rings and halve the tentacles or leave them whole.

3. Add the seafood to the stew, season to taste with salt and pepper, if using, re-cover and cook on high for 30 minutes, or until tender and cooked through. Remove and discard the bay leaf. Transfer to warmed serving bowls and drizzle with the remaining oil. Garnish with coriander leaves and serve immediately.

Variation

YOU COULD REPLACE THE RED MULLET WITH WHITE FISH SUCH AS COD, HALIBUT OR SEA BASS.

Per serving: 479 kcals | 18.1g fat | 3.5g sat fat | 20g carbs | 10g sugar | 4.5g fibre | 59.4g protein | 1.5g salt

STUFFED APPLES

This simple dessert is much healthier than apple pie, but just as delicious — and it is much less labour intensive.

SERVES 4   PREP: 20 MINUTES   COOK: 1½–3 HOURS

4 large cooking apples
175 g/6 oz soft light brown sugar
25 g/1 oz rolled oats
1 tsp ground cinnamon
55 g/2 oz butter, cut into small pieces
2 tbsp sultanas
25 g/1 oz pecan nuts or walnuts, roughly chopped
125 ml/4 fl oz water
20 ml/¾ fl oz double cream, whipped, to serve

1. Use a paring knife to cut the stem end out of each apple, then scoop out the core with a melon baller or teaspoon, leaving the base of the apple intact.

2. Put the sugar, oats, cinnamon and butter into a bowl and mix together with a fork. Add the sultanas and nuts and toss to mix well. Stuff the mixture into the apples, dividing it evenly.

3. Pour the water into the slow cooker, then carefully add the apples, standing them up in the base of the slow cooker. Cover and cook on high for about 1½ hours or on low for 3 hours. Serve the apples hot, topped with whipped cream.

41

Top Tip

THE FILLING IS ENOUGH FOR FOUR APPLES, BUT YOU CAN SCALE THE AMOUNT UP OR DOWN, AS LONG AS THE APPLES FIT IN YOUR SLOW COOKER.

Per serving: 514 kcals | 18.9g fat | 9g sat fat | 86.4g carbs | 69.6g sugar | 8.8g fibre | 2.9g protein | 0.2g salt

APPLE, PLUM AND ALMOND COMPOTE

A stewed fruit compote is a very versatile dish. The almond extract, an essential component, creates a wonderful flavour.

1.3 kg/3 lb cooking apples, peeled, cored and roughly chopped

600 g/1 lb 5 oz plums, stoned and quartered

50 g/1¾ oz soft brown sugar

1 tsp vanilla extract

1 tsp almond extract

50 g/1¾ oz flaked almonds, toasted, to decorate

1. Place the apples, plums, sugar, vanilla extract and almond extract in the slow cooker.

2. Cover the slow cooker and cook on high for 3 hours. Then stir the contents to break down any remaining chunks of apple.

3. Serve hot, warm or cold with a sprinkling of flaked almonds.

42

Top Tip

SERVE THIS WITH YOGURT OR PORRIDGE FOR BREAKFAST OR WITH ICE CREAM FOR AN EASY DESSERT.

Per serving: 254 kcals | 5.1g fat | 0.3g sat fat | 50.7g carbs | 39.5g sugar | 8.3g fibre | 3.4g protein | trace salt

Chapter 2

LOAD AND LEAVE

*Cook the convenient way and leave
your ingredients in the slow cooker for
a dish with a rich, full flavour.*

SPRING CHICKEN STEW WITH CHIVE DUMPLINGS

This warming one-pot meal is incredibly easy to make. The pearl barley and dumplings mean that no other accompaniments are needed.

SERVES 5   PREP: 30 MINUTES   COOK: 4 HOURS

1 large onion, finely chopped
3 celery sticks, diced
2 garlic cloves, diced
3 leeks, chopped into thin rounds
8 skinless, boneless chicken thighs
70 g/2½ oz pearl barley
small bunch of fresh thyme
zest and juice of 1 lemon
500 ml/17 fl oz chicken stock
100 g/3½ oz frozen peas
1 small courgette, cut into thin crescents
50 g/1¾ oz baby spinach
salt and pepper (optional)

Dumplings
50 g/1¾ oz butter, softened
125 g/4½ oz self-raising flour
40 g/1½ oz Cheddar cheese, crumbled
1 tbsp finely chopped fresh chives
3–4 tbsp cold water

1. Place the onion, celery, garlic, leeks, chicken, pearl barley, thyme and lemon zest and juice in the slow cooker. Pour over the stock and season with salt and pepper, if using. Cover and cook on high for 3 hours.

2. Meanwhile, make the dumplings. Rub the butter into the flour and mix in the cheese and chives. Add just enough cold water to bring the mixture together to form a soft dough and divide the dough into 5–6 small dumplings.

3. Stir the peas, courgette and baby spinach into the stew. Add the dumplings to the surface, re-cover and cook on high for a further hour. Serve, sprinkled with pepper, if using.

47

Variation

DEPENDING ON THE TIME OF YEAR YOU CAN USE ROOT VEGETABLES AS AN ALTERNATIVE TO CELERY AND LEEKS.

Per serving: 518 kcals | 18.8g fat | 8.9g sat fat | 46.1g carbs | 6.3g sugar | 6.7g fibre | 40.5g protein | 2.4g salt

LAMB TAGINE

Slow cookers are ideal for tagines because steam rises up to the slow cooker lid and re-condenses before trickling back down into the stew.

SERVES 4   PREP: 20 MINUTES   COOK: 7 HOURS

950 g/2lb 2 oz shoulder or leg of lamb, cut into 2.5-cm/1-inch cubes

2 onions, roughly chopped

1 large knob of ginger, grated

3 garlic cloves, halved

2 tsp ground coriander

1 tsp ground cumin

1 tsp ground allspice

125 g/4½ oz medjool dates, stoned and halved

1 tbsp runny honey

400 g/14 oz canned chopped tomatoes

zest of 1 lemon, keeping some aside to garnish

1 whole cinnamon stick

150 ml/5 fl oz hot lamb stock

2 tbsp chopped fresh coriander, to garnish

600 g/1 lb 5 oz freshly prepared couscous, to serve

48

1. Place the lamb, onions, ginger, garlic, ground coriander, cumin, allspice and dates in the slow cooker. Drizzle over the honey and add the tomatoes and most of the lemon zest. Add the cinnamon stick and pour over the hot stock.

2. Cover the slow cooker and cook on low for 7 hours, until the lamb is falling apart. Add a little hot water to the tagine, if needed. Transfer to warmed plates, garnish with the remaining lemon zest and coriander and serve with the couscous.

Per serving: 772 kcals | 30.5g fat | 13g sat fat | 73.9g carbs | 31g sugar | 6.3g fibre | 53.7g protein | 0.6g salt

BOSTON BAKED BEANS

The long slow-cooking process creates a beautifully syrupy sauce in this dish, which is totally irresistible.

SERVES 4   PREP: 20 MINUTES, PLUS OVERNIGHT SOAKING   COOK: 8 HOURS 15 MINUTES

350 g/12 oz dried cannellini beans, soaked overnight, or for at least 5 hours
1 large onion, cut in half
2 bay leaves
100 ml/3½ fl oz maple syrup
70 g/2½ oz soft brown sugar
1 tbsp black treacle
1 tsp chilli flakes
1 tbsp Worcestershire sauce
1 tbsp Dijon mustard
200 g/7 oz bacon lardons or pork belly, cut into 2-cm/¾-inch pieces
150 ml/5 fl oz water
120 g/4 oz wholemeal toast (4 slices), to serve

1. Drain and rinse the beans, place in a saucepan, cover with fresh cold water and bring to the boil. Boil rapidly for at least 10 minutes, then remove the pan from the heat, drain the beans and rinse them again.

2. Put the beans in the slow cooker with the onion, bay leaves, syrup, sugar, treacle, chilli, Worcestershire sauce and mustard.

3. Stir the lardons into the mixture and add the water.

4. Cover the slow cooker and cook on low for 8 hours, until the beans are tender and the sauce is syrupy. If you can, stir the contents halfway through the cooking process. Remove the bay leaves, transfer to warmed bowls and serve immediately with wholemeal toast.

51

Top Tip

IF YOU LIKE SPICY FOOD, SPRINKLE IN A TOUCH MORE CHILLI FLAKES, OR IF YOU LOVE WORCESTERSHIRE SAUCE, INCREASE THE QUANTITY.

Per serving: 687 kcals | 14.9g fat | 4.8g sat fat | 110.7g carbs | 39.8g sugar | 16.1g fibre | 31.2g protein | 1.8g salt

SHREDDED BEEF AND PEARL BARLEY STEW

Enriched with porcini mushrooms, this stew has a bold, robust quality. Easy to make, it can also be frozen, so is brilliant for minimum-effort entertaining.

SERVES 6   PREP: 30 MINUTES, PLUS SOAKING   COOK: 7 HOURS 10 MINUTES

30 g/1 oz dried porcini mushrooms
350 ml/12 fl oz boiling water
1 kg/2 lb 4 oz rolled beef brisket
2 tbsp vegetable oil
2 medium onions, finely chopped
3 garlic cloves, sliced
½ tsp crushed dried chillies
30 g/1 oz butter
150 g/5½ oz pearl barley
3 sprigs of rosemary
500 ml/17 fl oz hot beef stock
salt and pepper (optional)
2 tbsp chopped fresh parsley, to garnish
mixed salad, optional, to serve

52

1. Soak the porcini in the boiling water for 30 minutes. Remove the mushrooms, reserving the liquid, and squeeze them dry in your hands. Finely chop the mushrooms and set aside.

2. Season the brisket well with salt and pepper, if using. Heat the oil in a large frying pan and, using tongs to steady the meat, brown the beef all over for about 6–8 minutes.

3. Place the onion, garlic, chillies, butter, pearl barley and porcini mushrooms in the slow cooker. Nestle the beef in the centre and add the rosemary sprigs. Pour the porcini water and beef stock around the meat. Cover and cook on high for 7 hours, or until the beef is really tender.

4. Just before serving, shred the brisket using two forks and return it to the pot, mixing it in well. Transfer the stew to shallow bowls, garnish with parsley and serve with a mixed salad, if liked.

Per serving: 421 kcals | 18g fat | 6.4g sat fat | 25.7g carbs | 2.2g sugar | 5.5g fibre | 40.4g protein | 1.2g salt

LOUISIANA COURGETTES

Use a mixture of green and yellow courgettes for added colour in this simple vegetable recipe, which can be served as a side dish for non-vegetarians.

SERVES 6   PREP: 20 MINUTES   COOK: 2½ HOURS

1 kg/2 lb 4 oz courgettes, thickly sliced

1 onion, finely chopped

2 garlic cloves, finely chopped

2 red peppers, deseeded and chopped

5 tbsp hot vegetable stock

4 tomatoes, peeled and chopped

25 g/1 oz butter, diced

salt and cayenne pepper (optional)

275 g/9¾ oz crusty bread, to serve

1. Place the courgettes, onion, garlic and red peppers in the slow cooker and season to taste with salt and cayenne pepper, if using. Pour in the stock and mix well.

2. Sprinkle the chopped tomatoes on top and dot with the butter. Cover and cook on high for 2½ hours until tender. Serve immediately with crusty bread.

54

Top Tip

YOU MIGHT NOT THINK OF COURGETTES AS SLOW COOKER VEGETABLES, BUT THEY WORK BECAUSE THE COURGETTE SKIN HOLDS THEM TOGETHER.

Per serving: 216 kcals | 5.9g fat | 2.7g sat fat | 35.2g carbs | 8.8g sugar | 4.9g fibre | 7.3g protein | 0.9g salt

TAKE IT SLOW

When slow cookers first became popular in the post-war years and then later in the seventies, their main attraction was their convenience. Women were leading more independent lives and slow cookers, which were designed to be left cooking all day, helped families to achieve a balance between work and home, which of course included having a low-maintenance, nutritious evening meal.

The attraction is the same today. It really is possible to cut, chop and slice your ingredients, put them in the slow cooker before you go to work and come back at the end of the day to the tempting aromas and flavours of a healthy meal.

FREE UP YOUR TIME

The novelty of a delicious home-cooked meal where the human involvement is only needed right at the beginning and the end of the process is a liberating experience. Some of the best slow-cooker meals that suit the 'load and leave' scenario are soups and stews, because the slow cooker will simmer on a low setting for long periods of time and that way of cooking suits these dishes perfectly. The steam produced during the process will condense on the lid, as with a traditional tagine or casserole, and then return to the pot, constantly recycling the heat around the ingredients.

PLANNING AHEAD

There is naturally some initial preparation work cutting up vegetables and meat, and it is also true for some dishes that if you fry onions and brown some types of meat before adding them to the slow cooker, then the flavours of the final meal will be fully maximized. However this should not detract from the convenience of the slow cooker, because most of these processes can be carried out the night before. Just put your cooked, chopped and browned ingredients into the slow cooker dish and cover and store it in the fridge overnight. Then take the dish out of the fridge and leave it for 20 minutes before turning the cooker on so it has reached the right temperature.

CLEVER TECHNOLOGY

Slow cookers need a minimum of supervision, and the technology adds to the convenience of the whole process. Once the dish has reached its full cooking time, most slow cookers shift to a 'warm' setting, so you arrive home and your evening meal is, quite literally, waiting for you. So all that's required is for you to add a few herbs and to have a plate and a knife and fork ready.

SALMON WITH DILL AND LIME

Slow cooking is so gentle that the delicate flavour of the salmon is retained in this simply cooked fish dish.

SERVES 4   PREP: 20 MINUTES   COOK: 4 HOURS

40 g/1½ oz butter, melted

1 onion, thinly sliced

450 g/1 lb potatoes, thinly sliced

100 ml/3½ fl oz hot fish stock or water

4 pieces skinless salmon fillet, about 140 g/5 oz each

juice of 1 lime

2 tbsp chopped fresh dill

salt and pepper (optional)

lime wedges from half a lime, to serve

1. Brush the base of the slow cooker with 1 tablespoon of the butter. Layer the onion and potatoes in the dish, sprinkling with salt and pepper, if using, between the layers. Add the stock and drizzle with 1 tablespoon of the butter. Cover and cook on low for 3 hours.

2. Arrange the salmon over the vegetables in a single layer. Drizzle the lime juice over, sprinkle with dill and salt and pepper, if using, and pour the remaining butter on top. Cover and cook on low for a further 1 hour, until the fish flakes easily.

3. Serve the salmon and vegetables on warmed plates with the juices spooned over and lime wedges on the side.

58

Top Tip

YOU CAN SERVE THIS DISH WITH FRENCH BEANS OR PEAS FOR AN ELEGANT LUNCH OR DINNER.

Per serving: 373 kcals | 17.2g fat | 6.6g sat fat | 23.7g carbs | 2.3g sugar | 3g fibre | 30.6g protein | 0.6g salt

MANGO BEEF IN LETTUCE CUPS

This tantalizing combination of fresh mango and beef, packed with sweet and spicy flavours, has its roots in the Orient.

SERVES 8   PREP: 20 MINUTES   COOK: 2 HOURS

675 g/1 lb 8 oz chuck steak, cut into 1-cm/½ -inch dice

1 tbsp cornflour

1 mango, peeled, stoned and diced

2 hot red chillies, deseeded and diced

2 tbsp soy sauce

2 tbsp mirin or other sweet white wine

2 tbsp soft brown sugar

1 tsp sesame oil

150 g/5½ oz cup-shaped lettuce leaves, to serve

1. Put the beef and the cornflour into the slow cooker and toss to coat the beef evenly. Add the mango and chillies and stir to mix. Add the soy sauce, mirin, sugar and oil and stir to mix well.

2. Cover and cook on high for about 1 hour, then set the lid slightly ajar and continue to cook on high for a further 1 hour, until the meat is tender and the sauce has thickened.

3. Transfer the meat to a serving bowl and serve with the lettuce leaves, so that diners can scoop some of the meat into a lettuce cup and wrap it up like a taco.

61

Top Tip

IF YOU ARE NOT KEEN ON SPICY FOOD, THEN YOU CAN OMIT THE CHILLI PEPPERS – THE DISH WORKS JUST AS WELL WITHOUT THEM.

Per serving: 206 kcals | 8.6g fat | 3g sat fat | 13.7g carbs | 10.9g sugar | 1g fibre | 17.4g protein | 0.7g salt

TURKEY AND RICE CASSEROLE

This is a great low-fat recipe if you're counting the calories, and the turkey is a refreshing change from chicken.

SERVES 4   PREP: 20 MINUTES   COOK: 2 HOURS 5 MINUTES

1 tbsp olive oil

500 g/1 lb 2 oz turkey breast, diced

1 onion, diced

2 carrots, diced

2 celery sticks, sliced

250 g/9 oz closed-cup mushrooms, sliced

175 g/6 oz long-grain rice, preferably Basmati

450 ml/15 fl oz hot chicken stock

salt and pepper (optional)

1. Heat the oil in a heavy-based frying pan, add the turkey and fry over a high heat for 3–4 minutes, until lightly browned.

2. Combine the onion, carrots, celery, mushrooms and rice in the slow cooker. Arrange the turkey on top, season well with salt and pepper, if using, and pour over the stock. Cover and cook on high for 2 hours.

3. Stir lightly with a fork to mix, adjust the seasoning to taste and serve immediately.

62

Top Tip

THE CASSEROLE IS DELICIOUS SERVED WITH SOY SAUCE OR CHILLI SAUCE.

Per serving: 378 kcals | 7.4g fat | 1.3g sat fat | 43.8g carbs | 4.4g sugar | 2.8g fibre | 35g protein | 1.3g salt

STEAK ROULADES WITH SPINACH AND FETA

Rolling steak around a flavoursome filling makes for an elegant presentation of a surprisingly simple dish.

SERVES 4   PREP: 20 MINUTES   COOK: 3–6 HOURS

4 chuck steaks, about 675 g/
1 lb 8 oz in total, pounded to a
thickness of 1 cm/½ inch

½ onion, diced

115 g/4 oz feta cheese, crumbled

30 g/1 oz stoned Kalamata olives,
chopped

4 small handfuls baby
spinach leaves

50 ml/2 fl oz beef stock or water

salt and pepper (optional)

a few sprigs of chopped fresh flat
leaf parsley, to garnish

1. Season the steaks on both sides with salt and pepper, if using. Top each steak with a quarter each of the onion, cheese, olives and spinach. Starting with one of the short sides, roll up the steaks into pinwheels and secure with kitchen string or wooden cocktail sticks.

2. Place the steak rolls in the slow cooker along with the stock, cover, and cook on high for about 3 hours or on low for 6 hours, until the meat is tender and cooked through. Slice the roulades and serve hot, garnished with the parsley.

65

Top Tip

CHUCK STEAK IS A SHOULDER CUT CONTAINING COLLAGEN – THIS IS DISTRIBUTED THROUGHOUT THE DISH AS IT COOKS, CREATING LOTS OF FLAVOUR.

Per serving: 379 kcals | 23.3g fat | 10.4g sat fat | 3.2g carbs | 1.8g sugar | 0.6g fibre | 37.2g protein | 1.3g salt

TRADITIONAL POT ROAST

The ultimate one-pot roast that produces tender meat, perfectly cooked vegetables and a memorable depth of flavour.

SERVES 4   PREP: 20 MINUTES   COOK: 9–10 HOURS

1 onion, finely chopped
4 carrots, sliced
4 baby turnips, sliced
4 celery sticks, sliced
2 potatoes, sliced
1 sweet potato, sliced
1.3–1.8 kg/3–4 lb topside of beef, in one piece
1 bouquet garni
300 ml/10 fl oz hot beef stock
salt and pepper (optional)

1. Place the onion, carrots, turnips, celery, potatoes and sweet potato in the slow cooker and stir to mix well.

2. Rub the beef all over with salt and pepper, if using, then place on top of the bed of vegetables. Add the bouquet garni and pour in the stock. Cover and cook on low for 9–10 hours, until the beef is cooked to your liking. Remove the bouquet garnis and serve immediately.

67

Top Tip

IT'S A SIMPLE TASK TO THICKEN THE COOKING JUICES IN THE POT ROAST WITH CORNFLOUR BEFORE SERVING.

Per serving: 630 kcals | 15.2g fat | 5.8g sat fat | 33.9g carbs | 8.9g sugar | 6.5g fibre | 91.7g protein | 1.6g salt

SUMMER VEGETABLE CASSEROLE

This dish uses fresh summer vegetables infused with slow-cooked flavour. You can easily replace the cubed potatoes with new potatoes.

SERVES 4   PREP: 20 MINUTES   COOK: 7 HOURS

500 g/1 lb 2 oz potatoes, cubed
2 courgettes, cubed
2 red peppers, deseeded and cubed
2 red onions, sliced
2 tsp mixed dried herbs
250 ml/9 fl oz hot vegetable stock
salt and pepper (optional)

1. Layer all the vegetables in the slow cooker, sprinkling with the herbs and salt and pepper, if using, between the layers.

2. Pour over the stock. Cover and cook on low for 7 hours. Transfer to warmed serving bowls, sprinkle with black pepper, if using, and serve immediately.

68

Variation

YOU CAN ADD OTHER SUMMER VEGETABLES THAT ARE IN SEASON TO VARY THE RECIPE.

Per serving: 150 kcals | 1g fat | 0.3g sat fat | 32.4g carbs | 7.5g sugar | 5.8g fibre | 4.8g protein | 0.6g salt

TURKEY HASH

This is a great-tasting combination as the slightly sweet, nutty flavour of the squash complements the rich turkey.

SERVES 4   PREP: 15 MINUTES   COOK: 7 HOURS 5 MINUTES

1 tbsp olive oil
500 g/1 lb 2 oz turkey mince
1 large red onion, diced
550 g/1 lb 4 oz butternut squash, diced
2 celery sticks, sliced
500 g/1 lb 2 oz potatoes, diced
3 tbsp Worcestershire sauce
2 bay leaves
salt and pepper (optional)

1. Heat the oil in a frying pan, add the turkey and fry over a high heat, stirring, until broken up and lightly browned.

2. Place all the vegetables in the slow cooker then add the turkey and pan juices. Add the Worcestershire sauce and bay leaves and season with salt and pepper, if using. Cover and cook on low for 7 hours. Remove the bay leaves, transfer to warmed serving bowls and serve immediately.

71

Variation

RED AND GREEN PEPPERS CAN ALSO BE ADDED WITH THE OTHER VEGETABLES.

Per serving: 404 kcals | 14.1g fat | 3.2g sat fat | 44.5g carbs | 7.2g sugar | 6.4g fibre | 27.8g protein | 0.6g salt

HAM COOKED IN CIDER

A gammon joint makes a great mid-week roast and cooking it in this way means that the meat stays moist.

SERVES 6   PREP: 20 MINUTES   COOK: 8 HOURS, PLUS STANDING

1 kg/2 lb 4 oz boneless gammon joint
1 onion, halved
4 cloves
6 black peppercorns
1 tsp juniper berries
1 celery stick, chopped
1 carrot, sliced
1 litre/1¾ pints medium cider
black pepper (optional)
salad with 3 medium tomatoes, 2 small red onions and 125 g/4½ oz rocket, to serve

72

1. Place a trivet or rack in the slow cooker, if you like, and stand the gammon on it. Otherwise, just place the gammon in the slow cooker. Stud each onion half with two of the cloves and add to the slow cooker with the peppercorns, juniper berries, celery and carrot.

2. Pour in the cider, cover and cook on low for 8 hours, until the meat is tender.

3. Remove the gammon from the cooker and place on a board. Tent with foil and leave to stand for 10–15 minutes. Discard the cooking liquid and flavourings.

4. Cut off any rind and fat from the gammon joint and carve into slices. Transfer to serving plates and serve immediately with black pepper, if using, and the salad.

Top Tip

ANY COLD HAM LEFTOVERS WILL MAKE EXCELLENT SANDWICHES.

Per serving: 253 kcals | 12.7g fat | 4.2g sat fat | 4.7g carbs | 2.7g sugar | 1.3g fibre | 30.4g protein | 3.7g salt

RICE PUDDING

Creamy rice pudding flavoured with vanilla is delicious served simply with ground cinnamon. You can also top with a little maple syrup before serving.

SERVES 4   PREP: 15 MINUTES   COOK: 2¼ HOURS – 2 HOURS 20 MINUTES

140 g/5 oz short-grain rice
1 litre/1¾ pints milk
115 g/4 oz caster sugar
1 tsp vanilla extract
1 tsp ground cinnamon, for dusting

1. Rinse the rice well under cold running water and drain thoroughly. Pour the milk into a large heavy-based saucepan, add the sugar and bring to the boil, stirring constantly. Sprinkle in the rice, stir well and simmer gently for 10–15 minutes. Transfer the mixture to a heatproof dish and cover with foil.

2. Stand the dish on a trivet in the slow cooker and pour in enough boiling water to come about one third of the way up the side of the dish. Cover and cook on high for 2 hours.

3. Remove the dish from the slow cooker and discard the foil. Stir the vanilla extract into the rice, then spoon it into warmed bowls. Lightly dust with cinnamon and serve immediately.

74

Top Tip

YOU CAN MAKE THE RICE PUDDING IN ADVANCE IN RAMEKINS AND THEN EITHER PUT IT INTO THE OVEN FOR 10 MINUTES OR EAT IT COLD – IT'S JUST AS DELICIOUS!

Per serving: 393 kcals | 8.3g fat | 4.7g sat fat | 69g carbs | 41.5g sugar | 1.3g fibre | 10.2g protein | 0.3g salt

SWEET POTATO, APPLE AND RAISIN COMPOTE

This is an unusual combination for a fruit compote, but the sweet potato is delicious and adds body. Use fresh nutmeg as this improves the taste.

SERVES 6   PREP: 15 MINUTES   COOK: 3 HOURS

550 g/1 lb 4 oz sweet potatoes (around 4), peeled and cut into 3-cm/1¼-inch cubes

800 g/1 lb 12 oz apples (around 4), peeled and cut into 4-cm/1½-inch cubes

100 g/3½ oz raisins

200 ml/7 fl oz apple juice

1 tbsp runny honey

½ tsp freshly ground nutmeg

¼ tsp ground cloves

70 g/2½ oz pecan nuts, roughly chopped, to decorate

30 ml/1 fl oz double cream, whipped, to serve

1. Place the sweet potatoes, apples, raisins, apple juice, honey, nutmeg and cloves in the slow cooker. Cover and cook on high for 3 hours. Once cooked, stir the ingredients gently to combine them.

2. Put the compote in bowls, decorate with the pecan nuts and serve with whipped cream.

77

Variation

IF YOU ARE PREPARING A SEASONAL DESSERT, ADD DRIED CRANBERRIES AND ORANGE ZEST FOR A FESTIVE TWIST.

Per serving: 322 kcals | 11.2g fat | 2.3g sat fat | 56.6g carbs | 33.8g sugar | 6.3g fibre | 3.5g protein | 0.1g salt

Chapter 3

COMFORT

*Slow cooker dishes have the
potential to soothe, console, reassure
and simply make you feel good.*

LAMB STEW WITH ARTICHOKE AND ROSEMARY

This comforting stew is given a lift with the inclusion of artichoke hearts, rosemary and lemon, which sit perfectly with the slow-cooked lamb.

SERVES 4   PREP: 20 MINUTES   COOK: 5½ HOURS

1 tbsp olive oil

900 g/2 lb lamb shoulder, cut into 3-cm/1¼-inch cubes

1 large onion, sliced

4 garlic cloves, thinly sliced

300 ml/10 fl oz red wine

2 tbsp red wine vinegar

1 tbsp tomato purée

10 g/¼ oz chopped fresh rosemary

400 g/14 oz canned chopped tomatoes

400 g/14 oz artichoke hearts, chargrilled or in brine

zest and 2 tbsp lemon juice from 1 lemon

400 g/14 oz canned cannellini beans, drained

salt and pepper (optional)

2 tbsp chopped fresh parsley, to garnish

wholegrain mustard mash, made from 1 kg/2 lb 4 oz potatoes and 8 tsp mustard, to serve

80

1. Heat the oil in a large frying pan over a high heat. Brown the lamb in batches, using tongs to steady the meat, for about 8–10 minutes until the cubes are well coloured. Transfer to the slow cooker.

2. Add a little more oil to the pan, if needed, add the onion and cook over a low heat for 3–4 minutes, until softened, adding the garlic for the final minute. Add the wine and let it reduce by half, for around 5–6 minutes, before adding the onion, garlic and wine to the slow cooker.

3. Add the vinegar, tomato purée, rosemary and tomatoes to the slow cooker and mix well. Season with salt and pepper, if using. Re-cover and cook on high for 4 hours.

4. Add the artichokes, lemon zest and juice and the beans to the slow cooker. Cover and cook on high for an hour. Transfer to warmed serving bowls, garnish with the parsley and serve with mustard mash.

Per serving: 992.7 kcals | 52.4g fat | 21.2g sat fat | 64g carbs | 9.7g sugar | 14.3g fibre | 49.7g protein | 1.1g salt

MEXICAN CHICKEN BOWLS

This all-in-one chicken dish is perfect for easy entertaining — the bulk of the work is done by the slow cooker, and the garnish makes it even more inviting.

SERVES 4   PREP: 10 MINUTES   COOK: 4–5 HOURS

8 boneless chicken thighs, skin removed, trimmed of fat

6 large shallots, quartered

4 garlic cloves, peeled

400 g/14 oz canned black beans

200 g/7 oz canned sweetcorn, drained (drained weight 150 g/5½ oz)

200 g/7 oz brown rice

½ tsp cayenne pepper

1 green pepper, deseeded and sliced

1 green chilli, sliced

juice of 1 lime

300 ml/10 fl oz vegetable stock

150 ml/5 fl oz boiling water

salt and pepper (optional)

2 small avocados, sliced, to garnish

2 tbsp roughly chopped fresh coriander, to garnish

100 ml/3½ fl oz soured cream, to serve

1. Place the chicken, shallots, garlic, beans, sweetcorn, rice, cayenne pepper, green pepper and chilli in the slow cooker. Squeeze over the lime juice and pour over the stock. Season with salt and pepper, if using. Cover and cook on high for 4–5 hours, until the rice is perfectly soft.

2. Stir through the boiling water to loosen the stew.

3. Transfer to warmed bowls, garnish with avocado and coriander and serve with sour cream.

83

Top Tip

BUY GOOD-QUALITY BROWN RICE, BECAUSE THEN THE GRAINS WILL RETAIN THEIR SHAPE DURING THE COOKING PROCESS.

Per serving: 706 kcals | 25.5g fat | 7.3g sat fat | 64.9g carbs | 7.1g sugar | 14.2g fibre | 51.9g protein | 1.3g salt

TOMATO AND LENTIL SOUP

Simple yet satisfying and flavoured with the warm spices of cumin and coriander, basic lentils can be easily transformed into a healthy bowl of soup.

SERVES 4   PREP: 20 MINUTES   COOK: 3¾–4¼ HOURS

2 tbsp sunflower oil
1 onion, chopped
1 garlic clove, finely chopped
2 celery sticks, chopped
2 carrots, chopped
1 tsp ground cumin
1 tsp ground coriander
175 g/6 oz red or yellow lentils
1 tbsp tomato purée
1.2 litres/2 pints vegetable stock
400 g/14 oz canned chopped tomatoes
1 bay leaf
salt and pepper (optional)
4 tbsp crème fraîche and 175 g/6 oz toasted crusty bread, to serve

84

1. Heat the oil in a saucepan. Add the onion and garlic and cook over a low heat, stirring occasionally, for 5 minutes, until softened. Stir in the celery and carrots and cook, stirring occasionally, for a further 4 minutes. Stir in the ground cumin and coriander and cook, stirring, for 1 minute, then add the lentils.

2. Mix the tomato purée with a little of the stock in a small bowl and add to the pan with the remaining stock, the tomatoes and bay leaf. Bring to the boil, then transfer to the slow cooker. Stir well, cover and cook on low for 3½–4 hours.

3. Remove and discard the bay leaf. Transfer the soup to a food processor or blender and process until smooth. Season to taste with salt and pepper, if using. Ladle into warmed soup bowls, top each with a tablespoon of crème fraîche and a sprinkling of pepper, if using, and serve immediately with toasted crusty bread.

Top Tip

RED LENTILS CAN HAVE DEBRIS IN THEM, SO RINSE THEM WELL UNDER RUNNING WATER.

Per serving: 451 kcals | 16.5g fat | 5.7g sat fat | 62.3g carbs | 8g sugar | 8.3g fibre | 17.1g protein | 3.6g salt

SALMON CHOWDER

Salmon and fennel are the perfect match in this recipe, which would make a delicious starter for a special dinner with friends.

SERVES 4   PREP: 25 MINUTES   COOK: 3 HOURS 55 MINUTES – 4 HOURS

15 g/½ oz butter
1 tbsp sunflower oil
1 onion, finely chopped
1 leek, finely chopped
1 fennel bulb, finely chopped, feathery tops reserved
280 g/10 oz potatoes, diced
750 ml/1¼ pints fish stock
450 g/1 lb salmon fillet, skinned and cut into cubes
300 ml/10 fl oz milk
150 ml/5 fl oz single cream
2 tbsp chopped fresh dill
salt and pepper (optional)

1. Melt the butter with the oil in a saucepan. Add the onion, leek and fennel and cook over a low heat, stirring occasionally, for 5 minutes. Add the potatoes and cook, stirring occasionally, for a further 4 minutes, then pour in the stock and season to taste with salt and pepper, if using. Bring to the boil, then transfer to the slow cooker. Cover and cook on low for 3 hours, until the potatoes are tender.

2. Meanwhile, chop the fennel fronds and set aside. Add the salmon to the slow cooker, pour in the milk and stir gently. Re-cover and cook on low for 30 minutes, until the fish flakes easily.

3. Gently stir in the cream, dill and the reserved fennel fronds, re-cover and cook for a further 10–15 minutes, until heated through. Taste and adjust the seasoning, adding salt and pepper, if using. Serve immediately.

87

Variation

FOR A FAMILY SUPPER THE SALMON CAN BE REPLACED BY ANY FIRM WHITE FISH.

Per serving: 513 kcals | 32.4g fat | 12.4g sat fat | 27.7g carbs | 10g sugar | 4g fibre | 29.5g protein | 2.3g salt

CHICKEN SOUP WITH TAGLIATELLE

Tales that this soup can cure a cold may be far-fetched but a proper chicken soup is one of the most soul-warming recipes you can make.

SERVES 4   PREP: 25 MINUTES   COOK: 5 HOURS 35 MINUTES

1 onion, diced
2 celery sticks, diced
2 carrots, diced
1 kg/2 lb 4 oz oven-ready chicken
700 ml/1¼ pints hot chicken stock
115 g/4 oz dried egg tagliatelle
salt and pepper (optional)
2 tbsp chopped fresh dill, plus 1 tbsp to garnish

1. Place the onion, celery and carrots in the slow cooker. Season the chicken all over with salt and pepper, if using, and place on top. Pour over the stock. Cover and cook on low for 5 hours.

2. Leaving the juices in the slow cooker, carefully lift out the chicken and remove the meat from the carcass, discarding the bones and skin. Cut the meat into bite-sized pieces.

3. Skim the excess fat from the juices, then return the meat to the slow cooker. Turn the setting to high.

4. Bring a large saucepan of water to the boil, lightly salted if you are using salt. Add the tagliatelle, bring back to the boil and cook for 8–10 minutes, or until the tagliatelle is tender but still firm to the bite. Drain well.

5. Stir the dill into the slow cooker, cover and cook on high for a further 20 minutes. Garnish with extra dill, add a sprinkling of pepper, if using, and serve immediately.

Per serving: 325 kcals | 7.5g fat | 2.1g sat fat | 26.2g carbs | 3.7g sugar | 2.5g fibre | 36.9g protein | 1.9g salt

MACARONI CHEESE WITH TOASTED BREADCRUMBS

This classic comfort food dish is a breeze to make in the slow cooker. A toasted breadcrumb topping cooked on the hob adds a welcome crunch.

SERVES 4   PREP: 20 MINUTES   COOK: 2 HOURS 20 MINUTES – 4 HOURS 20 MINUTES

1 tbsp vegetable oil, for brushing
25 g/1 oz butter
2 tbsp plain flour
150 ml/5 fl oz vegetable stock
450 ml/16 fl oz evaporated milk
1½ tsp mustard powder
⅛ – ¼ tsp cayenne pepper
1 tsp salt
175 g/6 oz Gruyère cheese, grated
175 g/6 oz fontina cheese, grated
55 g/2 oz freshly grated Parmesan cheese
350 g/12 oz dried elbow macaroni
350 ml/12 fl oz water

Topping
2 thick slices (about 200 g/7 oz) French bread
25 g/1 oz butter

1. Line the slow cooker with foil and brush with a little oil.

2. Melt the butter in a large frying pan or saucepan over a medium–high heat. Whisk in the flour and cook for 1 minute. Reduce the heat to medium and slowly add the stock, evaporated milk, mustard, cayenne pepper and salt. Cook, stirring, for about 3–5 minutes, until thick. Add all the cheeses and whisk until melted. Add the macaroni and stir to mix well. Transfer to the slow cooker.

3. Add the water and stir to mix. Cover and cook on high for 2 hours or on low for 4 hours, until the macaroni is tender.

4. To make the topping, process the bread in a food processor to make crumbs. Melt the butter in a large frying pan over a medium heat until bubbling. Add the breadcrumbs and cook, stirring frequently, for about 5 minutes, until toasted and golden brown.

5. Serve hot, topped with the breadcrumbs.

91

Variation

INTRODUCE EXTRA COLOUR AND TEXTURE BY ADDING VEGETABLES SUCH AS BROCCOLI, CAULIFLOWER, PEAS OR SWEETCORN WITH THE MACARONI.

Per serving: 1186 kcals | 58.1g fat | 32.8g sat fat | 109.1g carbs | 18.8g sugar | 4.1g fibre | 56.1g protein | 5.1g salt

CHICKEN AND MUSHROOM STEW

Slow cooking creates tender, rich mushrooms and a superb flavour. This is ideal for a family supper and also a great choice for a dinner with friends.

SERVES 4   PREP: 20 MINUTES   COOK: 7 HOURS 35 MINUTES

15 g/½ oz unsalted butter
2 tbsp olive oil
1.8 kg/4 lb skinless chicken portions
2 red onions, sliced
2 garlic cloves, finely chopped
400 g/14 oz canned chopped tomatoes
2 tbsp chopped fresh flat-leaf parsley
6 fresh basil leaves, torn
1 tbsp sun-dried tomato purée
150 ml/5 fl oz red wine
225 g/8 oz mushrooms, sliced
salt and pepper (optional)

92

1. Heat the butter and oil in a heavy-based frying pan. Add the chicken, in batches if necessary, and cook over a medium–high heat, turning frequently, for 10 minutes, until golden brown all over. Using a slotted spoon, transfer the chicken to the slow cooker.

2. Add the onions and garlic to the frying pan and cook over a low heat, stirring occasionally, for 10 minutes, until golden. Add the tomatoes with their can juices, stir in the parsley, basil, tomato purée and wine and season with salt and pepper, if using. Bring to the boil, then pour the mixture over the chicken.

3. Cover the slow cooker and cook on low for 6½ hours. Stir in the mushrooms, re-cover and cook on high for 30 minutes, until the chicken is tender and the vegetables are cooked through. Taste and adjust the seasoning if necessary and serve immediately.

Variation

YOU CAN USE DIFFERENT TYPES OF MUSHROOMS – OTHER IDEAS ARE SHIITAKE, CHANTERELLES, CHESTNUT AND OYSTER MUSHROOMS.

Per serving: 669 kcals | 26.1g fat | 7.4g sat fat | 12.9g carbs | 7.6g sugar | 2.1g fibre | 90.2g protein | 1.7g salt

CHUNKY BEEF CHILLI

Chunks of beef, onions, garlic and green pepper are cooked with chilli to give just the right amount of kick to this satisfying dish.

SERVES 4   PREP: 25–30 MINUTES, PLUS OVERNIGHT SOAKING   COOK: 9¼ HOURS

250 g/9 oz dried red kidney beans, soaked overnight, or for at least 5 hours
600 ml/1 pint water
2 garlic cloves, chopped
5 tbsp tomato purée
1 small green chilli, chopped
2 tsp ground cumin
2 tsp ground coriander
600 g/1 lb 5 oz chuck steak, diced
1 large onion, chopped
1 large green pepper, deseeded and sliced
salt and pepper (optional)
4 tbsp soured cream, to serve

1. Drain and rinse the beans, place in a saucepan, add enough water to cover and bring to the boil. Boil rapidly for 10 minutes, then remove from the heat and drain and rinse again. Place the beans in the slow cooker and add the cold water.

2. Mix the garlic, tomato purée, chilli, cumin and coriander together in a large bowl. Add the steak, onion and green pepper and mix to coat evenly.

3. Place the meat and vegetables on top of the beans, cover and cook on low for 9 hours, until the beans and meat are tender. Stir and season to taste with salt and pepper, if using.

4. Transfer to warmed serving bowls and top with a tablespoon of soured cream. Serve immediately.

95

Top Tip

SERVE THE CHILLI WITH RICE, TORTILLA CHIPS AND GUACAMOLE FOR A SATISFYING MEAL.

Per serving: 472 kcals | 14.6g fat | 6g sat fat | 39g carbs | 7.1g sugar | 12.6g fibre | 484g protein | 0.2g salt

TAGLIATELLE WITH TUNA

When you just want a simple and tasty meal, this is the perfect choice.
Serve with some crusty bread, a crisp salad and maybe a glass of white wine.

SERVES 4   PREP: 20 MINUTES   COOK: 2 HOURS 10 MINUTES

200 g/7 oz dried egg tagliatelle
400 g/14 oz canned tuna steak
in oil, drained
1 bunch spring onions, sliced
175 g/6 oz frozen peas
2 tsp hot chilli sauce
600 ml/1 pint hot chicken stock
115 g/4 oz Cheddar cheese,
grated
salt and pepper (optional)

1. Bring a large saucepan of lightly salted water to the boil. Add the pasta, return to the boil and cook for 2 minutes, until the pasta ribbons are loose. Drain.

2. Break up the tuna into bite-sized chunks and place in the slow cooker with the pasta, spring onions and peas. Season to taste with salt and pepper, if using.

3. Add the chilli sauce to the stock and pour over the ingredients in the slow cooker. Sprinkle the grated cheese over the top. Cover and cook on low for 2 hours. Serve immediately on warmed plates, topped with black pepper, if using.

96

Top Tip

THICKER PASTAS SUCH AS TAGLIATELLE CAN LAST A LONGER TIME IN THE SLOW COOKER THAN FINER VARIETIES, WHICH CAN BECOME MUSHY.

Per serving: 486 kcals | 19g fat | 7.7g sat fat | 43.3g carbs | 4.6g sugar | 4.2g fibre | 32.8g protein | 2.7g salt

SPICY PULLED PORK

Slow cooking creates pork that's deliciously moist, tender and full of flavour for the ultimate sandwich that everyone will love.

SERVES 4   PREP: 25 MINUTES   COOK: 8 HOURS

2 onions, sliced
1.5 kg/3 lb 5 oz boned and rolled pork shoulder
2 tbsp demerara sugar
2 tbsp Worcestershire sauce
1 tbsp American-style mustard
2 tbsp tomato ketchup
1 tbsp cider vinegar
salt and pepper (optional)
4 hamburger buns, to serve

1. Put the onions in the slow cooker and place the pork on top. Mix the sugar, Worcestershire sauce, mustard, ketchup and vinegar together and spread all over the surface of the pork. Season to taste with salt and pepper, if using. Cover and cook on low for 8 hours.

2. Remove the pork from the slow cooker and use two forks to pull it apart into shreds.

3. Skim any excess fat from the juices and stir a little juice into the pork. Serve in hamburger buns, with the remaining juices for spooning over.

99

Top Tip

ADD A GENEROUS TABLESPOON OF PAPRIKA TO GIVE YOUR MINI HOG ROAST MORE SPICE.

Per serving: 733 kcals | 30.1g fat | 10.5g sat fat | 37.9g carbs | 15.6g sugar | 1.8g fibre | 73.5g protein | 3.2g salt

PUMPKIN RISOTTO

This stunning risotto, enriched with nutritious and delicious pumpkin, is a satisfying vegetarian main course for a festive autumn meal.

SERVES 4   PREP: 20 MINUTES   COOK: 1 HOUR 55 MINUTES

2 tbsp olive oil

1 shallot, finely chopped

1 garlic clove, finely chopped

280 g/10 oz arborio rice

125 ml/4 fl oz dry white wine

1.2 litres/2 pints vegetable stock

425 g/15 oz canned pumpkin purée

1 tbsp finely chopped fresh sage

½ tsp salt

¼ tsp pepper

pinch of nutmeg

25 g/1 oz butter

175 g/6 oz freshly grated Parmesan cheese

1. Heat the oil in a large frying pan over a medium–high heat. Add the shallot and garlic and cook, stirring, for about 5 minutes, until soft. Add the rice and cook, stirring, for 1 minute. Add the wine and cook for a further 3 minutes, until the liquid is absorbed. Transfer the mixture to the slow cooker.

2. Stir in the stock, pumpkin purée, sage, salt, pepper and nutmeg. Cover and cook on high for about 1½ hours, until the rice is tender. Stir in the butter, re-cover and cook for a further 15 minutes. Stir in two thirds of the cheese and serve immediately, with the remaining cheese sprinkled over.

100

Per serving: 611 kcals | 25.6g fat | 12.7g sat fat | 69.4g carbs | 4.9g sugar | 5.4g fibre | 21.9g protein | 5.2g salt

GO SLOW AND INDULGE YOURSELF

The meals we eat give us energy and valuable nutrients, but the right meal also has the potential to make us feel positive and optimistic. A smooth bowl of tomato soup, for example, will soothe you if you are feeling under the weather, a warming meat stew will warm you up on a cold winter's day — you can even share a plate of divine chocolate cookies with friends on a lazy afternoon as a sublime slow cooker treat!

WARMING FARE

It's not just in the middle of winter that a hearty plate of stew, a chilli with some kick or a smooth vegetarian risotto might appeal. After a long day at work, we look for something to satisfy our hunger and help us relax and destress. So if a comforting slow-cooked meal is ready when we get home, then all the better.

TRADITIONAL DISHES

The food we eat has strong associations and certain dishes can transport us back to a particular time and place, perhaps the familiar taste of a dish that your mother used to make or one associated with sociable family meals. Some comfort meals such as macaroni cheese or tuna pasta might evoke childhood teatimes and remind you of old friends, or a delicious apple crumble served with custard might have formed the much-loved conclusion of Sunday lunches with all the family.

UPLIFTING MEALS

If you need a meal to lift your spirits and recharge your energy levels, there are also restorative slow cooker options that can put you back on the straight and narrow. Chicken Tortilla Soup, for example, will give you a hearty boost, or Pork Stuffed with Apples combines sweet fruit, salty ham and crumbly, nutty Gorgonzola for a memorable meal you can take your time over. You see, going slow has never had so much to offer!

INDULGENCE

It's hard to resist an indulgent treat, but indulgence doesn't have to be sweet – it can also be full of goodness. This is all about how food makes you feel. Chicken, pork, mashed potato, sweetcorn, avocado, chilli sauce and melting Cheddar cheese are just a few ingredients that, used in the right way with other ingredients that complement them, can cover both indulgent and nutritious bases. The indulgence of a slow cooker meal is often multiplied by the lack of preparation work. A dish might have a long cooking time, but your work could simply be limited to putting the ingredients in the slow cooker and serving it up with delicious (or indulgent) accompaniments of your choice.

CHICKEN TORTILLA SOUP

This healthy soup is a hearty first course or a light meal in a bowl and will be a sure-fire favourite in the cold winter months.

SERVES 6   PREP: 20 MINUTES   COOK: 4¼–8¼ HOURS

1 tbsp vegetable oil
1 onion, diced
1 tsp chilli powder
1 tsp salt
½ tsp ground cumin
2 tbsp tomato purée
900 ml/1½ pints chicken stock
400 g/14 oz canned chopped tomatoes, with juice
1 green chilli, deseeded and finely chopped
450 g/1 lb bone-in, skinless chicken thighs
40 g/1½ oz tortilla chips, broken into small pieces

To serve
1 ripe avocado, diced
1 tbsp chopped fresh coriander
1 lime, cut into wedges
125 g/4½ oz tortilla chips

1. Heat the oil in a large frying pan over a medium–high heat. Add the onion and cook, stirring occasionally, for about 5 minutes, until soft. Add the chilli powder, salt, cumin and tomato purée and cook, stirring, for a further 1 minute. Add one third of the stock to the pan and bring to the boil, stirring and scraping up any brown bits from the base of the pan.

2. Transfer the mixture to the slow cooker. Add the remaining stock, the tomatoes, chilli, chicken and tortilla chips, then cover and cook on low for about 4 hours or on high for 8 hours, until the chicken is cooked through and very tender.

3. Lift out the chicken using a slotted spoon, remove and discard the bones and shred the meat. Return the chicken to the slow cooker, cover and heat on high for about 5 minutes, until heated through. Serve hot, accompanied by diced avocado, chopped coriander, lime wedges and tortilla chips.

Per serving: 314 kcals | 16.7g fat | 2.8g sat fat | 28.7g carbs | 4.7g sugar | 4.6g fibre | 14.4g protein | 2.7g salt

PORK STUFFED WITH APPLES

This is a great taste combination with sweet apples, salty ham and pungent Gorgonzola to offset the natural richness of the pork.

SERVES 4   PREP: 25 MINUTES   COOK: 4–7 HOURS

1 large apple, peeled, cored and sliced

125 ml/4 fl oz apple juice or water

4 boneless pork chops, about 2.5 cm/1 inch thick

4 slices prosciutto

115 g/4 oz Gorgonzola cheese

salt and pepper (optional)

600 g/1 lb 5oz mashed potato, to serve

1. Place half of the apple slices in the base of the slow cooker and add the apple juice.

2. Butterfly the pork chops by laying each chop flat on a chopping board and, pressing down on it with the flat of your hand to keep it in place, cutting through the centre horizontally, leaving one side attached like a hinge. Loosely wrap in clingfilm and gently pound with a meat mallet to a thickness of about 2 cm/¾ inch.

3. Open the flattened and butterflied chops like books and place on the chopping board. Layer each chop with a slice of prosciutto, a quarter of the cheese and a quarter of the remaining apple slices. Fold closed and secure with wooden cocktail sticks.

4. Season the stuffed chops all over with salt and pepper, if using, and place in the slow cooker on top of the apple slices. Cover and cook on high for about 4 hours or on low for about 7 hours, until the meat is cooked through. Serve hot with the mashed potato.

107

Top Tip

THIS DISH IS ALSO A SUCCESS SERVED WITH BAKED POTATOES OR MASHED SWEET POTATOES WITH CRISP GREEN VEGETABLES.

Per serving: 560 kcals | 18.9g fat | 9.6g sat fat | 37g carbs | 10.7g sugar | 3g fibre | 57.9g protein | 3g salt

DOUBLE CHOCOLATE COOKIES

Although they look more like brownies than traditional round cookies, these luxurious chocolate treats will win plenty of fans.

MAKES ABOUT 18   PREP: 20 MINUTES, PLUS COOLING   COOK: 3 HOURS

125 g/4½ oz plain flour
85 g/3 oz cocoa powder
½ tsp baking powder
¼ tsp salt
115 g/4 oz unsalted butter, softened, plus 10 g/¼ oz unsalted butter for greasing
100 g/3½ oz sugar
1 large egg
1 tsp vanilla extract
25 g/1 oz plain chocolate chips

108

1. Generously grease the inside of the slow cooker with butter.

2. Put the flour, cocoa powder, baking powder and salt into a medium-sized bowl and mix to combine. Put the butter and sugar into a large bowl and cream together. Add the egg and vanilla extract and beat well together. Gradually beat in the flour mixture until well incorporated. Stir in the chocolate chips.

3. Using a rubber spatula, scrape the batter into the prepared slow cooker and smooth the top. Cover and cook on low for 2½ hours. Set the lid slightly ajar and continue to cook on low for a further 30 minutes.

4. Leaving the cookie in the ceramic insert, remove it from the slow cooker and transfer to a wire rack to cool for 30 minutes. Turn the cookie out onto the rack and leave to cool for a further 30 minutes before slicing it into 5-cm/2-inch pieces. Serve at room temperature.

Per cookie: 121 kcals | 7.2g fat | 4.4g sat fat | 14.4g carbs | 6.2g sugar | 2g fibre | 2.2g protein | 0.1g salt

APPLE CRUMBLE

This simple dessert will fill your house with the sweet smell of autumn, and it's the perfect way to end a meal on a chilly evening.

SERVES 6   PREP: 25 MINUTES   COOK: 3–5 HOURS

100 g/3½ oz sugar
1 tbsp cornflour
1 tsp ground cinnamon
¼ tsp ground nutmeg
6 large cooking apples, peeled, cored and chopped
2 tbsp lemon juice
vanilla ice cream, to serve, optional

Topping
60 g/2¼ oz plain flour
75 g/2¾ oz soft light brown sugar
3 tbsp granulated sugar
pinch of salt
40 g/1½ oz unsalted butter, cut into small pieces
60 g/2¼ oz rolled oats
85 g/3 oz pecan nuts or walnuts, roughly chopped

110

1. Put the sugar, cornflour, cinnamon and nutmeg into the slow cooker and stir to combine. Add the apples and lemon juice and toss to coat well.

2. To make the topping, put the flour, brown sugar, granulated sugar and salt into a large mixing bowl and mix to combine. Using two knives, cut the butter into the flour mixture until it resembles coarse crumbs. Add the oats and nuts and toss until well combined.

3. Sprinkle the topping evenly over the apple mixture, cover and cook on high for about 2 hours or on low for about 4 hours, until the apples are soft. Set the lid ajar and cook for a further 1 hour, or until the topping is crisp. Serve warm, topped with vanilla ice cream, if using.

Top Tip

SPREADING APRICOT JAM ON THE APPLES WILL MAKE YOUR CRUMBLE TASTE MUCH FRUITIER.

Per serving: 474 kcals | 16.7g fat | 4.5g sat fat | 82.8g carbs | 59.3g sugar | 5.7g fibre | 4.3g protein | 0.2g salt

Chapter 4

GLOBAL

You can travel all around the
world with the help of your slow
cooker, without packing your bags.

HUNGARIAN PORK GOULASH

This Hungarian staple has the distinctive flavours of sweet paprika, peppers and tomato. Top the goulash with sour cream for a classic finish.

SERVES 4   PREP: 20 MINUTES   COOK: 8 HOURS 10 MINUTES

2 tsp olive oil

2 kg/4 lb 8 oz off-the-bone pork shoulder joint, skin off, fat left on

2 red onions, finely sliced

3 garlic cloves, sliced

1 tbsp mild smoked paprika, plus a little extra to garnish

2 tsp caraway seeds

1 small bunch fresh oregano, leaves picked

4 peppers, mixed colours

400 g/14 oz canned plum tomatoes

100 ml/3½ fl oz vegetable stock

4 tbsp red wine vinegar

salt and pepper (optional)

2 tbsp chopped fresh parsley, to garnish

100 g/3½ oz soured cream, to serve

175 g/6 oz freshly cooked rice, to serve

1. Heat the oil in a large frying pan over a high heat. Using tongs, sear the pork shoulder for 6–8 minutes, until the meat takes on some colour and the fat renders down.

2. Add the onions, garlic, paprika and caraway seeds to the slow cooker and place the pork shoulder joint on top. Nestle the oregano and peppers around the sides of the pork. Add the tomatoes, stock and vinegar. Season with salt and pepper, if using. Cover and cook on high for 8 hours, or until the pork is tender and falling apart.

3. Slice the pork and deseed and slice the whole peppers.

4. Transfer to warmed plates, garnish with paprika and parsley and serve with the soured cream and rice.

114

Per serving: 941 kcals | 46.6g fat | 16.8g sat fat | 31.5g carbs | 10.4g sugar | 6.9g fibre | 96.5g protein | 3.5g salt

VIETNAMESE BEEF NOODLE SOUP

You'll find it easier to cut the very thin slices needed for this dish if you place the meat in the freezer for 15 minutes before slicing.

SERVES 4   PREP: 25 MINUTES   COOK: 5 HOURS 35 MINUTES – 8 HOURS 35 MINUTES

2 litres/3½ pints beef stock

1 onion, quartered

5-cm/2-inch piece of fresh ginger, thickly sliced lengthways

2 cinnamon sticks

3 whole cloves

2 star anise or 1 tsp fennel seeds

2 tbsp Thai fish sauce

1 tsp sugar

450 g/1 lb dried rice noodles

225 g/8 oz beef sirloin, very thinly sliced

salt (optional)

Accompaniments, to serve.

115 g/4 oz beansprouts

lime wedges, cut from 1 lime

1 tbsp chopped fresh herbs, including basil, coriander and/ or mint

4 spring onions, thinly sliced

2 hot chillies, thinly sliced

1. Put the stock, onion, ginger, cinnamon sticks, cloves, star anise, fish sauce and sugar into the slow cooker and stir to combine. Cover and cook on high for 5 hours or on low for 8 hours. Add salt to taste, if using.

2. Pour the liquid through a fine-meshed sieve or a colander lined with muslin and discard the solids. Return the clear soup to the slow cooker and heat on high for about 30 minutes, until very hot, or transfer to a large saucepan and bring to a slow boil over a medium–high heat.

3. Just before serving, cook the noodles according to the packet instructions.

4. Place a few slices of beef in the base of each of four soup bowls and ladle the soup over to lightly cook the beef. Add some noodles to each bowl. Serve immediately with the accompaniments set out in small bowls for diners to help themselves.

Top Tip

CALLED 'PHO' IN VIETNAM, THIS BROTH IS TRADITIONALLY COOKED FOR HOURS, SOMETIMES DAYS, SO THE SLOW COOKING METHOD IS A PERFECT FIT.

Per serving: 563 kcals | 8.1g fat | 3.4g sat fat | 100.6g carbs | 5.6g sugar | 3.3g fibre | 21.1g protein | 7.4g salt

ITALIAN BREAD SOUP WITH GREENS

This healthy, vegetable-packed soup plumps up as it cooks, creating a rich, thick soup that makes the world feel a better place.

SERVES 4   PREP: 20 MINUTES   COOK: 4 HOURS 35 MINUTES – 8 HOURS 35 MINUTES

2 tbsp olive oil

1 onion, diced

1 leek, halved lengthways and thinly sliced

2 litres/3½ pints vegetable stock

200 g/7 oz kale, chopped

2 celery sticks, diced

2 carrots, diced

1 tsp crumbled dried oregano

1½ tsp salt

½ tsp pepper

200 g/7 oz day-old cubed sourdough bread

30 g/1 oz freshly grated Parmesan cheese, to garnish

118

1. Heat the oil in a large frying pan over a medium–high heat. Add the onion and leek and sauté for about 5 minutes, until soft.

2. Transfer the mixture to the slow cooker and add the stock, kale, celery, carrots, oregano, salt and pepper. Cover and cook on high for about 4 hours or on low for 8 hours.

3. Add the bread to the soup, cover and cook on high, stirring occasionally, for about 30 minutes, until the bread breaks down and thickens the soup.

4. Serve hot, garnished with the cheese.

Variation

TURN THE SOUP INTO A ONE-DISH MEAL BY ADDING A CAN OF CANNELLINI BEANS ALONG WITH THE VEGETABLES.

Per serving: 317 kcals | 13.6g fat | 4.4g sat fat | 42.8g carbs | 8.4g sugar | 5.2g fibre | 11.8g protein | 8.1g salt

EASY CHINESE CHICKEN

This great-tasting recipe can be served simply with steamed rice or as part of a meal with the addition of a quickly cooked stir-fried vegetable selection.

SERVES 2   PREP: 20 MINUTES   COOK: 4 HOURS 5 MINUTES

2 tsp grated fresh ginger

4 garlic cloves, finely chopped

2 star anise

150 ml/5 fl oz Chinese rice wine or medium dry sherry

2 tbsp dark soy sauce

1 tsp sesame oil

5 tbsp water

4 skinless chicken thighs or drumsticks

2 shredded spring onions, to garnish

700 g/1 lb 9oz cooked rice, to serve

1. Mix together the ginger, garlic, star anise, rice wine, soy sauce, sesame oil and water in a bowl. Place the chicken in a saucepan, add the spice mixture and bring to the boil.

2. Transfer to the slow cooker, cover and cook on low for 4 hours, or until the chicken is tender and cooked through.

3. Remove and discard the star anise. Transfer the chicken to warmed serving plates, garnish with the shredded spring onions and serve immediately with the rice.

121

Top Tip

THIS IS A STRAIGHTFORWARD RECIPE TO PREPARE FOR A WEEKDAY SUPPER.

Per serving: 731 kcals | 7.9g fat | 1.8g sat fat | 107g carbs | 0.9g sugar | 2.1g fibre | 33.1g protein | 2.4g salt

SAUSAGE AND BEAN CASSOULET

Here is slow cooking at its best, a variation on the famous regional French casserole, named after the pot it's traditionally cooked in.

SERVES 4   PREP: 20 MINUTES   COOK: 6 HOURS 10 MINUTES

2 tbsp sunflower oil

2 onions, chopped

2 garlic cloves, finely chopped

115 g/4 oz streaky bacon, chopped

500 g/1 lb 2 oz pork sausages

400 g/14 oz canned haricot, red kidney or black-eyed beans, drained and rinsed

2 tbsp chopped fresh parsley

150 ml/5 fl oz hot beef stock

122

To serve

4 slices (around 400 g/14 oz) French bread

55 g/2 oz Gruyère cheese, grated

1. Heat the oil in a heavy-based frying pan. Add the onions and cook over a low heat, stirring occasionally, for 5 minutes, until softened. Add the garlic, bacon and sausages and cook, stirring and turning the sausages occasionally, for a further 5 minutes.

2. Using a slotted spoon, transfer the mixture from the frying pan to the slow cooker. Add the beans, parsley and stock, then cover and cook on low for 6 hours.

3. Shortly before serving, preheat the grill. Place the bread slices on the grill rack and lightly toast on one side under the preheated grill. Turn the slices over, sprinkle with the grated cheese and place under the grill until just melted.

4. Serve the cassoulet with the bread slices immediately.

Top Tip

USE GOOD-QUALITY SAUSAGES TO ACHIEVE THE VERY BEST RESULTS.

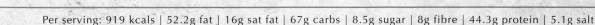

Per serving: 919 kcals | 52.2g fat | 16g sat fat | 67g carbs | 8.5g sugar | 8g fibre | 44.3g protein | 5.1g salt

ASPARAGUS AND SPINACH RISOTTO

Cooking risotto in this way removes the tedious stirring that is usually associated with this classic Italian dish.

SERVES 4   PREP: 20 MINUTES   COOK: 2 HOURS 35 MINUTES

2 tbsp olive oil

4 shallots, finely chopped

280 g/10 oz arborio rice

1 garlic clove, crushed

100 ml/3½ fl oz dry white wine

900 ml/1½ pints vegetable stock

200 g/7 oz asparagus spears

200 g/7 oz baby spinach leaves

40 g/1½ oz freshly grated Parmesan cheese

salt and pepper (optional)

1. Heat the oil in a frying pan, add the shallots and fry over a medium heat, stirring, for 2–3 minutes. Add the rice and garlic and cook for a further 2 minutes, stirring. Add the wine and allow it to boil for 30 seconds.

2. Transfer the rice mixture to the slow cooker, add the stock and season to taste with salt and pepper, if using. Cover and cook on high for 2 hours, or until most of the liquid is absorbed.

3. Cut the asparagus into 4-cm/1½-inch lengths. Stir into the rice, then spread the spinach over the top. Replace the lid and cook on high for a further 30 minutes, until the asparagus is just tender and the spinach is wilted.

4. Stir in the spinach with the cheese, then adjust the seasoning to taste, and serve immediately in warmed bowls.

125

Top Tip

ARBORIO RICE IS USED HERE BECAUSE IT GIVES THE RISOTTO A DISTINCTIVE AND APPEALING CREAMINESS.

Per serving: 422 kcals | 11.3g fat | 3.6g sat fat | 65.7g carbs | 2.7g sugar | 4.4g fibre | 11.5g protein | 2.6g salt

BEEF AND CHIPOTLE BURRITOS

Chipotle peppers are smoked, dried jalapeño chillies, used in Mexican cooking for centuries – they add the heat to this spicy beef filling for tortillas.

SERVES 4   PREP: 25 MINUTES, PLUS SOAKING   COOK: 4 HOURS 10 MINUTES

1 tbsp olive oil

1 onion, sliced

600 g/1 lb 5 oz chuck steak

1 dried chipotle pepper, soaked in boiling water for 20 minutes

1 garlic clove, crushed

1 tsp ground cumin

400 g/14 oz canned chopped tomatoes

8 large tortillas

salt and pepper (optional)

4 tbsp soured cream and 125 g/4½ oz green salad, to serve

126

1. Heat the oil in a pan and fry the onion for 3–4 minutes until golden. Tip into the slow cooker and arrange the beef on top. Drain and chop the chipotle. Sprinkle the chipotle pepper, garlic, cumin, tomatoes, salt and pepper, if using, over the meat.

2. Cover and cook on low for 4 hours, until the meat is tender.

3. Warm the tortillas. Remove the beef and shred with a fork. Divide between the tortillas and spoon over the tomato sauce. Wrap, and serve with the soured cream and green salad.

Variation

REPLACE THE TORTILLAS WITH ENCHILADAS, TACOS, NACHOS OR QUESADILLAS.

Per serving: 678 kcals | 23.1g fat | 8.7g sat fat | 70.6g carbs | 8.4g sugar | 3.5g fibre | 44.1g protein | 1.4g salt

INTERNATIONAL GO SLOW

In our multi-cultural society, our most favourite meals are not necessarily those with their roots close to home. Many national classics have travelled all over the world and have become an essential part of different food cultures. The Italian risotto, the Spanish paella, the French bouillabaisse and the Hungarian pork goulash, for example, are all recognized and enjoyed internationally.

These dishes and many more can be created in a slow cooker, with all their original flavours and a minimum of fuss. The recipes in this chapter show us how a slow cooker can create the meals that we already love and maybe introduce a few new ones, allowing us to travel gastronomically from Europe to China and from North Africa to New England.

GLOBAL RECIPES IN A SLOW COOKER

It's not a challenge to find slow cooker recipes with global impact. From goulash to tagines and pulled pork to cassoulet, every cuisine has a slow cooking genre.

Recipes based on stews or soups probably have the longest food history of all, and transfer easily to a slow cooker, where the long, slow cooking process mirrors the simmering of a soup on the hob or a stew gently cooking in an oven. Hungary and Spain are just a couple of the countries with national recipes that translate beautifully to the slow cooker. The bouillabaisse, for example, is simplified from the French classic, but still results in a delicious stew characterized by saffron, oregano, tomatoes and succulent seafood. Slow cooking also suits the Spanish-style Vegetarian Paella, which is cooked in the slow cooker until the rice is tender and the stock absorbed, in the same way as you would cook the paella in a pan over a low heat.

The ingredients for Italian Bread Pudding would normally be combined in a mould, surrounded by boiling water and baked in the oven. The process is the same in the slow cooker, but the panettone, milk, cream, sugar and lemon now have two and a half hours to meld with the Marsala into a delicious end-of-meal offering.

FROM EUROPE TO THE ORIENT

It's not just classic European meals that you can enjoy with your slow cooker. The flavours of Africa, America and the Orient also have a valid place, where the slow cooking process tenderizes the meat or chicken and infuses the flavours of garlic, ginger, soy sauce as well as chilli (Korea) and fish sauce (Thailand and Vietnam) perfectly.

So, you see, you really can travel home and eat your fill, exploring the world from your dining room table, with your trusty slow cooker doing all the work.

NEW ENGLAND CLAM CHOWDER

Many recipes for this fish soup exist up and down the east coast of America — some are creamy while others use tomatoes for colour and flavour.

SERVES 4   PREP: 20 MINUTES   COOK: 4 HOURS 5 MINUTES

25 g/1 oz butter
1 onion, finely chopped
2 potatoes, cut into cubes
1 large carrot, diced
400 ml/14 fl oz fish stock or water
280 g/10 oz canned clams, drained
275 ml/9 fl oz double cream
salt and pepper (optional)
chopped fresh parsley, to garnish
175 g/6 oz fresh crusty bread, to serve

1. Melt the butter in a frying pan, add the onion and fry over a medium heat for 4–5 minutes, stirring, until golden.

2. Transfer the onion to the slow cooker with the potatoes, carrot, stock and salt and pepper, if using. Cover and cook on high for 3 hours.

3. Add the clams and the cream to the slow cooker and stir to mix evenly. Cover and cook for a further hour.

4. Adjust the seasoning to taste. Transfer to warmed serving bowls, sprinkle with parsley and serve immediately with crusty bread.

131

Variation

WHEN SERVING THE CHOWDER, YOU CAN ALSO ADD PIECES OF FRIED BACON TO THE TOP OF EACH DISH.

Per serving: 668 kcals | 41g fat | 24.6g sat fat | 50g carbs | 4.6g sugar | 4.6g fibre | 24.7g protein | 2.1g salt

MOROCCAN SPICED BEEF STEW

Heady spices and sweet dried apricots come together for an exotic twist on beef stew.

SERVES 6   PREP: 20 MINUTES   COOK: 6 HOURS 10 MINUTES – 9 HOURS 10 MINUTES

2 tbsp vegetable oil
1 onion, diced
1½ tsp salt
½ tsp pepper
2 tsp ground cumin
½ tsp ground cinnamon
½ tsp ground ginger
225 ml/8 fl oz red wine
675 g/1 lb 8 oz chuck steak, cut into 5-cm/2-inch pieces
130 g/4¾ oz dried apricots, diced
2 tbsp honey
125 ml/4 fl oz water
chopped fresh coriander, to garnish
900 g/2 lb cooked couscous, to serve

132

1. Heat the oil in a large frying pan. Add the onion and cook, stirring, for about 5 minutes, until soft. Add the salt, pepper, cumin, cinnamon and ginger and cook, stirring, for a further 1 minute.

2. Add the wine, bring to the boil and cook for 1 minute, scraping up any sediment from the base of the pan. Transfer the mixture to the slow cooker.

3. Add the beef, apricots, honey and water and stir to mix. Cover and cook on high for 6 hours or on low for 9 hours, until the meat is very tender.

4. Serve hot with couscous, garnished with coriander.

Variation

TO INCREASE THE VEGETABLE CONTENT, ADD A SMALL SQUASH, CUT INTO MEDIUM CHUNKS, TO THE SLOW COOKER WITH THE BEEF.

Per serving: 499 kcals | 13.1g fat | 3.9g sat fat | 57.6g carbs | 18.5g sugar | 4.3g fibre | 30.7g protein | 1.7g salt

VEGETARIAN PAELLA

A delicious vegetarian version of the Spanish classic. If you include fish and seafood in your diet, you could add cooked prawns just before serving.

SERVES 6   PREP: 25 MINUTES   COOK: 2¾–3¼ HOURS

4 tbsp olive oil

1 onion, sliced

2 garlic cloves, finely chopped

1 litre/1¾ pints hot vegetable stock

large pinch of saffron threads, lightly crushed

1 yellow pepper, deseeded and sliced

1 red pepper, deseeded and sliced

1 large aubergine, diced

225 g/8 oz paella or risotto rice

450 g/1 lb tomatoes, peeled and chopped

115 g/4 oz chestnut mushrooms, sliced

115 g/4 oz French beans, halved

400 g/14 oz canned borlotti beans, drained and rinsed

salt and pepper (optional)

1. Heat the oil in a large frying pan. Add the onion and garlic and cook over a low heat, stirring occasionally, for 5 minutes, until softened. Put 3 tablespoons of the hot stock into a small bowl and stir in the saffron, then set aside to infuse.

2. Add the peppers and aubergine to the pan and cook, stirring occasionally, for 5 minutes. Add the rice and cook, stirring constantly, for 1 minute, until the grains are coated with oil and glistening. Pour in the remaining stock and add the tomatoes, mushrooms, French beans and borlotti beans. Stir in the saffron mixture and season to taste with salt and pepper, if using.

3. Transfer the mixture to the slow cooker, cover and cook on low for 2½–3 hours, until the rice is tender and the stock has been absorbed. Transfer to warmed serving plates and serve immediately.

135

Top Tip

A SOFT-GRAINED RICE SUCH AS BOMBA IS USED IN SPAIN – THIS ABSORBS THE STOCK WITHOUT BECOMING CREAMY OR STICKY.

Per serving: 330 kcals | 11g fat | 2g sat fat | 50.5g carbs | 9.2g sugar | 9.5g fibre | 8.4g protein | 1.6g salt

THAI BEEF CURRY

Enriched with coconut milk and peanut butter, this simple curry will transport you to Southeast Asia.

SERVES 4   PREP: 20 MINUTES   COOK: 5–9 HOURS

75 g/2¾ oz Thai red curry paste

175 ml/6 fl oz unsweetened coconut milk

50 g/1¾ oz soft dark brown sugar

1 tbsp Thai fish sauce

75 g/2¾ oz smooth peanut butter

900 g/2 lb chuck steak, cut into 2.5-cm/1-inch dice

2 potatoes, diced

125 ml/4 fl oz beef stock or water

fresh basil leaves, cut into ribbons, to garnish

700 g/1lb 9 oz steamed rice, to serve

1. Put the curry paste, coconut milk, sugar, fish sauce and peanut butter into the slow cooker and stir to combine. Add the beef, potatoes and stock and stir to coat in the mixture.

2. Cover and cook on high for about 4 hours or on low for 8 hours, then set the lid slightly ajar and cook for a further 1 hour, or until the beef is very tender and the sauce has thickened slightly. Serve hot, garnished with basil, with the steamed rice.

136

Top Tip

THE CREAMY COCONUT MILK TONES DOWN THE HEAT OF THE CURRY.

Per serving: 941 kcals | 38.8g fat | 17.4g sat fat | 87.3g carbs | 17.1g sugar | 4.2g fibre | 60.1g protein | 2.2g salt

EASY BOUILLABAISSE WITH GARLIC MAYONNAISE

This simplified version of the French classic is sure to impress. Feel free to add or substitute other types of fish or shellfish.

SERVES 4   PREP: 30 MINUTES   COOK: 2½-4½ HOURS

Bouillabaisse

pinch of saffron threads
1 tbsp hot water
2 tbsp olive oil
1 onion, diced
3 garlic cloves, finely chopped
2 celery sticks, finely chopped
2 tsp crumbled, dried oregano
1 tsp salt
¼ – ½ tsp crushed dried red pepper flakes
350 ml/12 fl oz dry white wine
400 g/14 oz passata
400 g/14 oz canned chopped tomatoes, with juice
12 small clams, scrubbed
12 mussels, scrubbed and debearded
450 g/1 lb white fish fillet, such as halibut, cut into 5-cm/2-inch pieces
225 g/8 oz raw prawns, peeled and deveined
2 tbsp finely chopped fresh parsley, to garnish

Garlic mayonnaise

2 garlic cloves, finely chopped
½ tsp salt
125 ml/4 fl oz mayonnaise

1. Place the saffron in a small bowl and cover with the hot water. Heat the oil in a large frying pan over a medium–high heat. Add the onion and garlic and cook, stirring, for about 5 minutes, until soft. Add the celery, oregano, salt and red pepper flakes, then add the wine. Bring to the boil and cook, stirring, for about 8 minutes, until the liquid is reduced by half. Transfer the mixture to the slow cooker.

2. Stir in the saffron and its soaking water, passata and tomatoes with their can juices. Cover and cook on high for about 2 hours or on low for about 4 hours.

3. Discard any clams or mussels with broken shells and any that refuse to close when tapped. Add the fish, prawns, clams and mussels to the slow cooker, cover and cook on high for a further 10–15 minutes, until the fish and prawns are cooked through and the clams and mussels have opened, discarding any that still remain closed.

4. To make the garlic mayonnaise, mash the garlic and salt together with a fork to make a paste. Stir in the mayonnaise. To serve, ladle some broth into four serving bowls, then add some of the fish and shellfish. Top each serving with a dollop of the garlic mayonnaise, garnish with parsley and serve immediately.

Per serving: 649 kcals | 34.4g fat | 5.2g sat fat | 20.2g carbs | 10.8g sugar | 2.5g fibre | 47.6g protein | 4.3g salt

KOREAN BRAISED BEEF RIBS

You'll end up with meltingly tender meat in this classic recipe. Ask your butcher to cut the ribs into 7.5-cm/3-inch lengths for easy serving.

SERVES 6   PREP: 20 MINUTES, PLUS MARINATING   COOK: 6–9 HOURS

1 onion, diced

3 garlic cloves, finely chopped

1 tbsp finely chopped fresh ginger

2 tbsp soy sauce

2 tbsp soft dark brown sugar

2 tbsp mirin or other sweet white wine

1 tbsp sesame oil

1 tsp chilli paste

1.25 kg/2 lb 12 oz bone-in beef short ribs

2 small potatoes, cubed

2 carrots, cubed

3 spring onions, thinly sliced, to garnish

1 tbsp toasted sesame seeds, to garnish

700 g/1 lb 9 oz steamed rice, to serve

1. Put the onion, garlic, ginger, soy sauce, sugar, mirin, oil and chilli paste into a bowl large enough to hold the meat and stir to combine. Add the ribs and turn to coat in the mixture. Cover and place in the refrigerator to marinate for at least 2 hours or overnight.

2. Place the beef, together with the marinade, in the slow cooker. Add the potatoes and carrots and stir to mix. Cover and cook on high for about 6 hours or on low for about 9 hours, until the meat is tender and falling off the bone.

3. Serve hot, garnished with the spring onions and sesame seeds, with steamed rice.

141

Top Tip

CALLED 'GALBI JIM' IN KOREA, THE DISH RELIES ON THE STEWED BONE MARROW FROM THE SHORT RIBS FOR ITS RICH FLAVOUR.

Per serving: 521 kcals | 19.5g fat | 7.3g sat fat | 51.5g carbs | 9g sugar | 2.5g fibre | 31.6g protein | 1.2g salt

ITALIAN BREAD PUDDING

A great variation on traditional bread and butter pudding – panettone is an Italian fruit loaf available mainly at Christmas.

SERVES 6   PREP: 20 MINUTES, PLUS COOLING AND CHILLING   COOK: 2 HOURS 35 MINUTES

10 g/¼ oz unsalted butter, for greasing
6 slices panettone
3 tbsp Marsala
300 ml/10 fl oz milk
300 ml/10 fl oz single cream
100 g/3½ oz caster sugar
grated rind of ½ lemon
¹⁄₁₆ tsp ground cinnamon
3 large eggs, lightly beaten

1. Grease a 1-litre/1¾ -pint pudding basin with butter. Place the panettone on a deep plate and sprinkle with the Marsala.

2. Pour the milk and cream into a pan and add the sugar, lemon rind and cinnamon. Gradually bring to the boil over a low heat, stirring until the sugar has dissolved. Remove the pan from the heat and leave to cool slightly, then pour the mixture onto the eggs, beating constantly.

3. Place the panettone in the prepared basin, pour in the egg mixture and cover with foil. Stand the basin on a trivet in the slow cooker and pour in enough boiling water to come about one third of the way up the side of the basin. Cover and cook on high for 2½ hours, until set.

4. Carefully remove the basin from the slow cooker and discard the foil. Leave to cool, then chill in the refrigerator until required. Run a knife around the inside of the basin, then turn out the bread pudding onto a serving dish. Serve immediately.

Variation

YOU CAN REPLACE THE PANETTONE WITH ANY SWEET FRUIT BREAD OR BRIOCHE, IF YOU PREFER.

Per serving: 438 kcals | 22.5g fat | 11.1g sat fat | 49.2g carbs | 34.2g sugar | 2.6g fibre | 9.6g protein | 0.3g salt

Chapter 5

WOW-FACTOR

These striking, impressive and memorable slow cooker dishes are certain to keep your guests talking.

RED THAI CURRY WITH SALMON AND LIME

This flavoursome Thai curry couldn't be easier, because the slow cooker does all the work. Serve with black rice for a sophisticated, elegant finish.

SERVES 4   PREP: 15 MINUTES   COOK: 2 HOURS

600 g/1 lb 5 oz salmon steaks, skinned and cut into 2–3-cm/ ¾-1¼-inch pieces

3 tbsp red curry paste

400 ml/14 fl oz full fat coconut milk

1 tbsp fish sauce

1 tbsp soft brown sugar

200 g/7 oz green beans, topped with the tails left on

1 green chilli, halved lengthways

4-cm/1½-inch piece of fresh ginger, finely grated

100 g/3½ oz frozen peas

juice of 1 lime

3 tbsp chopped fresh coriander, to garnish

700 g/1 lb 9 oz freshly cooked black rice, to serve

146

1. Place the salmon, red curry paste, coconut milk, fish sauce, sugar, green beans, chilli and ginger in the slow cooker.

2. Cover the slow cooker and cook on high for 1 hour 30 minutes. Add the peas and cook for a further 20–30 minutes, until the peas are tender. Taste the curry and add a touch more fish sauce, if liked.

3. Squeeze the lime juice over the curry and garnish with coriander. Serve immediately with black rice.

Per serving: 766 kcals | 45.7g fat | 24.7g sat fat | 54.4g carbs | 10.3g sugar | 6.2g fibre | 41.1g protein | 1.6g salt

TURKEY CHILLI WITH SWEET POTATOES

Add a can of black beans along with the sweet potatoes to feed more people and make this healthy chilli even more nutritious.

SERVES 4   PREP: 20 MINUTES   COOK: 4 HOURS 10 MINUTES – 8 HOURS 10 MINUTES

1 tbsp vegetable oil

1 onion, diced

675 g/1 lb 8 oz fresh turkey mince

70 g/2½ oz tomato purée

1 tbsp mild chilli powder

1 tsp ground cumin

2 canned chipotle chillies in adobo sauce, deseeded and diced, plus 2 teaspoons of the adobo sauce (or substitute 1 tsp ground chipotles)

1 tsp salt

400 g/14 oz canned chopped tomatoes

450 ml/16 fl oz chicken stock

1 large sweet potato (about 225 g/8 oz), diced

148

To serve

1 tbsp chopped fresh coriander

4 tbsp soured cream

40 g/1½ oz grated Cheddar cheese

diced avocado

finely chopped red onion

1. Heat the oil in a large frying pan. Add the onion and cook, stirring, for about 5 minutes, until soft. Add the turkey and cook, breaking up the meat with a wooden spoon, for about 4 minutes, until brown. Stir in the tomato purée, chilli powder, cumin, chillies and adobo sauce, and salt and cook for a further 1 minute.

2. Transfer the mixture to the slow cooker. Stir in the tomatoes, stock and sweet potato. Cover and cook on high for 4 hours or on low for 8 hours. Serve hot, accompanied by the coriander, soured cream, cheese, avocado and red onion.

Top Tip

TURKEY MINCE IS A HEALTHY AND LIGHTER ALTERNATIVE TO MINCED BEEF, LAMB OR PORK.

Per serving: 517 kcals | 29.5g fat | 8.4g sat fat | 28.1g carbs | 10.5g sugar | 7g fibre | 38.8g protein | 3.5g salt

CHICKEN IN RIESLING

This is a perfect dish for entertaining. Put it together, then leave it to cook while you make a dessert for your guests.

SERVES 6   PREP: 20–25 MINUTES   COOK: 5 HOURS 35 MINUTES – 6 HOURS 35 MINUTES

2 tbsp plain flour
1 chicken, weighing 1.6 kg/
3 lb 8 oz, cut into 8 pieces
55 g/2 oz unsalted butter
1 tbsp sunflower oil
4 shallots, finely chopped
12 button mushrooms, sliced
2 tbsp brandy
500 ml/17 fl oz Riesling wine
250 ml/9 fl oz double cream
salt and pepper (optional)
275 g/9¾ oz cooked green beans
and 225 g/8 oz peas,
to serve

1. Put the flour into a polythene bag and season to taste, if using salt and pepper. Add the chicken pieces, in batches, hold the top securely and shake well to coat. Transfer the chicken to a plate.

2. Heat half the butter with the oil in a heavy-based frying pan. Add the chicken pieces and cook over a medium–high heat, turning frequently, for 10 minutes, until golden all over. Using a slotted spoon, transfer them to a plate.

3. Wipe out the pan with kitchen paper, then return to a medium-high heat and melt the remaining butter. Add the shallots and mushrooms and cook, stirring constantly, for 3 minutes. Return the chicken to the frying pan and remove it from the heat. Warm the brandy in a small ladle, ignite and carefully pour it over the chicken, shaking the pan gently until the flames have died down.

4. Return the pan to the heat and pour in the wine. Bring to the boil over a low heat, scraping up any sediment from the base of the pan. Transfer to the slow cooker, cover and cook on low for 5–6 hours, until the chicken is tender and cooked through.

5. Transfer the chicken to a serving dish and keep warm. Skim off any fat from the surface of the cooking liquid and pour the liquid into a saucepan. Stir in the cream and bring just to the boil over a low heat and pour over the chicken. Serve immediately with the green vegetables.

151

Per serving: 946 kcals | 60.1g fat | 29.2g sat fat | 26.7g carbs | 12.4g sugar | 5.4g fibre | 50g protein | 0.3g salt

TURKEY BREAST WITH BACON, LEEKS AND PRUNES

When you have guests but a whole turkey is too much, this elegant dish with one turkey breast will feed up to eight people.

SERVES 8   PREP: 25 MINUTES   COOK: 5 HOURS 20 MINUTES – 9 HOURS 20 MINUTES, PLUS RESTING

115 g/4 oz bacon rashers

2 leeks, trimmed, white and light green parts, thinly sliced

1 skinless, bone-in turkey breast (about 1.8 kg/4 lb)

30 g/1 oz plain flour

1 tbsp olive oil, if needed

12 stoned prunes, halved (quartered, if large)

1 tsp crumbled dried thyme or 1 tbsp finely chopped fresh thyme

225 ml/8 fl oz chicken stock

salt and pepper (optional)

152

1. Heat a frying pan over a medium–high heat, then add the bacon and cook until just crisp. Remove from the pan, drain on kitchen paper, then chop or crumble into small pieces.

2. Add the leeks to the pan and cook in the bacon fat over a medium–high heat, stirring frequently, for about 5 minutes, or until soft.

3. Season the turkey with salt and pepper, if using, and dredge with the flour. If needed, add the oil to the pan, then add the turkey and cook on one side for 4–5 minutes, until brown. Turn and cook on the other side for a further 4–5 minutes, until brown.

4. Place the turkey in the slow cooker together with the leeks, bacon, prunes and thyme. Add the stock, cover and cook on high for about 5 hours or on low for about 9 hours.

5. Remove the turkey from the slow cooker and leave to rest for 5 minutes. Slice and serve with some of the sauce, including the prunes and bits of bacon, spooned over the top.

Top Tip

PRUNES GIVE A LITTLE MORE SWEETNESS TO THIS TURKEY DISH – THEY ALSO OFFER A RICH SUPPLY OF POTASSIUM AND VITAMIN C.

Per serving: 371 kcals | 8.6g fat | 2.2g sat fat | 15.7g carbs | 6.4g sugar | 1.6g fibre | 56g protein | 1.3g salt

HONEY-GLAZED DUCK LEGS

This elegant alternative to chicken legs creates an unforgettable dinner party dish with very little preparation.

SERVES 6   PREP: 15 MINUTES   COOK: 6 HOURS 20 MINUTES – 10 HOURS 20 MINUTES

6 duck legs
125 ml/4 fl oz chicken stock
3 tbsp red wine or white wine
115 g/4 oz clear honey
1 tbsp fresh thyme leaves
salt and pepper (optional)
700 g/1 lb 9 oz mashed potato,
to serve

1. Trim any excess skin or fat from the duck legs and season with salt and pepper, if using. Heat a large, heavy-based frying pan over a medium–high heat. When the pan is very hot, add the duck legs, in batches, if necessary, and cook on one side for about 4 minutes, until brown. Turn and cook on the other side for about 4 minutes, until brown. Transfer to the slow cooker.

2. Put the stock, wine, honey and thyme into a small bowl, stir to combine, then pour the mixture over the duck legs, turning to coat. Cover and cook on high for about 6 hours or on low for about 10 hours, until the duck is very tender. Serve hot with mashed potato.

155

Top Tip

YOU CAN DRIZZLE ANY EXCESS HONEY JUICES FROM THE SLOW COOKER OVER THE DUCK LEGS BEFORE SERVING.

Per serving: 362 kcals | 11.2g fat | 3.1g sat fat | 36.7g carbs | 17.3g sugar | 1.8g fibre | 26.9g protein | 1.3g salt

SLOW DOWN AND BE WOWED

You've had your slow cooker for a while and it has a regular place in your kitchen. Your family love the wafting aromas of meaty stocks and flavour-infused vegetables when they come home in the evening and the memorable meals that the slow cooker serves up. You love the convenience and the deep flavours of the soups, casseroles and pot roasts that have become part of your daily routine. So now it's time to raise your game, invite some guests around and impress them with your slow cooker regime.

SPEND TIME WITH YOUR GUESTS

When it comes to wow-factor, there is often some preparation involved. However the advantage of a slow cooker, even when preparing more ambitious recipes, is that many recipes don't have elaborate processes once the slow cooker has done its job. Think of Beef Ribs Braised in Red Wine – once they are in the slow cooker they just need serving up, perhaps with the addition of mashed potato, rice or polenta. This means you've still got plenty of time to spend chatting with your guests.

AWESOME DISHES

If you like to keep it simple, producing an amazing slow cooker meal doesn't have to eat up your precious time. Clams in Spicy Broth with Chorizo, for example, is a delicious offering for a light meal where the slow cooker does all the hard work – the clams are added for the final 15 minutes and, served with crusty bread, the clam-filled spectacle will be a sure-fire hit.

If your choice of dish needs a big wow-factor, try Butternut Squash and Goat's Cheese Enchiladas. Once the roasted squash is prepared, the sauce with onions, tomatoes and honey is layered in the slow cooker with the tortillas, squash and cheese. Two hours later you have your meal. Another option is Mini Chicken Pot Pies – the pot-pie mixture is prepared in the slow cooker, added to ramekins, topped with pastry and browned for 20 minutes (still leaving plenty of time for socialising).

SWEET AND SLOW

When it comes to desserts, the slow cooker offers a surprising number of options. Crème Brûlée is the sort of sweet, smooth dish that you might always zoom in on when dining out, but never think of making at home. But all you have to do is get out your slow cooker!

And who would think you could make a strawberry cheesecake in a slow cooker? Well you can – add the biscuit base and the fruity cheesecake mixture to a springform tin, put this in the slow cooker and leave it for two hours – afterwards letting it cool and then decorating with strawberries. Guaranteed to be a mealtime talking point!

BUTTERNUT SQUASH AND GOAT'S CHEESE ENCHILADAS

Roasting butternut squash caramelizes it, giving an enticing sweetness that balances out the spicy sauce and salty cheese.

SERVES 4   PREP: 35–40 MINUTES   COOK: 2 HOURS 50 MINUTES – 3 HOURS

1 large butternut squash, peeled and diced

4 tbsp olive oil

1 tsp salt

3 tsp ground cumin

1 large onion, diced

3 garlic cloves, finely chopped

1 tbsp hot or mild chilli powder

1 tbsp dried oregano

450g/1 lb canned chopped tomatoes or passata

1 tbsp clear honey

475 ml/16 fl oz vegetable stock

12 corn tortillas

225 g/8 oz soft, fresh goat's cheese

158

1. Preheat the oven to 200°C/400°F/Gas Mark 6. Line a baking tray with baking paper. Coat the squash with 2 tablespoons of the oil, sprinkle with half the salt and 1 teaspoon of the cumin. Place the squash on the tray and roast for 30–40 minutes, until soft and beginning to brown.

2. Heat the remaining oil in a large frying pan over a medium–high heat. Add the onion and garlic and cook, stirring, for about 5 minutes, until soft. Add the remaining cumin and salt, the chilli powder and the oregano and cook for a further 1 minute. Stir in the tomatoes, honey and stock, bring to the boil and cook for about 5 minutes. Purée the sauce in a food processor or blender.

3. Coat the base of the slow cooker with a little sauce. Make a layer of tortillas, tearing them if necessary, to cover the bottom of the slow cooker. Top the tortillas with a layer of the squash, a layer of cheese, a layer of sauce, then another layer of tortillas.

4. Layer again with squash, cheese and sauce. Finish with a layer of tortillas, sauce and the remaining cheese. Cover and cook on low for 2 hours, until the tortillas are soft and the cheese is melted and bubbling. Serve hot.

Variation

IF BUTTERNUT SQUASH IS HARD TO COME BY, SWEET POTATOES ARE A GOOD ALTERNATIVE.

Per serving: 362 kcals | 11.2g fat | 3.1g sat fat | 36.7g carbs | 17.3g sugar | 1.8g fibre | 26.9g protein | 1.3g salt

BEEF RIBS BRAISED IN RED WINE

This dish is incredibly tender and packed with flavour –
serve with mash or polenta to make the most of the rich sauce.

SERVES 6   PREP: 20 MINUTES   COOK: 7 HOURS 40 MINUTES – 10 HOURS 40 MINUTES

1.3 kg/3 lb bone-in beef short ribs

2 tbsp vegetable oil, plus extra, if needed

1 onion, diced

1 celery stick, diced

1 carrot, diced

1 tbsp tomato purée

3 fresh thyme sprigs

2 garlic cloves, finely chopped

3 tbsp plain flour

475 ml/16 fl oz red wine

225 ml/8 fl oz beef stock

1 bay leaf

salt and pepper (optional)

700 g/1 lb 9 oz mashed potato, to serve

160

1. Generously season the ribs with salt and pepper, if using. Heat the oil in a large, heavy-based frying pan over a medium–high heat. Add the ribs and cook, turning occasionally, for about 10 minutes, until brown on all sides. Transfer to the slow cooker.

2. Add more oil to the pan if needed and, when hot, add the onion, celery and carrot to the pan. Cook, stirring occasionally, for about 15 minutes, until the vegetables are soft. Add the tomato purée, thyme, garlic and flour and cook, stirring, for a further 1 minute.

3. Add the wine, bring to the boil and cook for a further 1–2 minutes, stirring and scraping up any sediment from the base of the pan. Reduce the heat to medium–low and simmer for 6–8 minutes, until the liquid is reduced by about half. Transfer to the slow cooker.

4. Stir in the stock, ½ teaspoon of salt and the bay leaf, cover and cook on high for 7 hours or on low for 10 hours, until the meat is very tender and falling from the bone. About 1–2 hours before the end of cooking, set the lid ajar, if desired, to allow the liquid to reduce and reach a thicker consistency.

5. Before serving, remove and discard the thyme and bay leaf. Serve hot with the mashed potato.

Per serving: 504 kcals | 22.1g fat | 8g sat fat | 29.5g carbs | 4g sugar | 2.7g fibre | 31g protein | 1.7g salt

MINI CHICKEN POT PIES

There's no better treat than a freshly made mini chicken pot pie and you don't have to spend hours over a hot stove for this version!

SERVES 6   PREP: 30 MINUTES, PLUS COOLING   COOK: 4 HOURS 40 MINUTES – 8 HOURS 40 MINUTES

3 tbsp butter
1 onion, diced
115 g/4 oz button mushrooms, diced
675 g/1 lb 8 oz skinless, boneless chicken, diced
1 carrot, diced
2 celery sticks, diced
1 tbsp fresh thyme leaves
2 tbsp plain flour
225 ml/8 fl oz milk
175 ml/6 fl oz chicken stock
1 tsp salt
½ tsp pepper
2 sheets ready-rolled puff pastry
10 g/¼ oz flour, for dusting

1. Melt 1 tablespoon of the butter in a large frying pan over a medium–high heat. Add the onion and cook, stirring, for about 5 minutes, until soft. Add the mushrooms and cook, stirring, for a further 3 minutes, or until the mushrooms are beginning to soften. Transfer the mixture to the slow cooker and add the chicken, carrot, celery and thyme.

2. Reduce the heat under the frying pan to medium, add the remaining butter and heat until melted. Whisk in the flour and cook, whisking constantly, until the mixture is lightly browned and begins to give off a nutty aroma. Whisk in the milk, stock, salt and pepper and continue to cook, stirring, for a further 5 minutes, or until the mixture begins to thicken.

163

3. Add the mixture to the slow cooker and stir to mix well. Cover and cook on high for about 4 hours or on low for about 8 hours, until the chicken is tender and the sauce has thickened. Divide the filling equally between 6 x 225-ml/8-fl oz ramekins.

4. Preheat the oven to 190°C/375°F/Gas Mark 5. Roll out the pastry on a lightly floured surface and cut out six rounds, each about 2.5 cm/1 inch larger in circumference than the ramekins. Top each filled ramekin with a pastry round, crimping the edges. Prick the pastry on each pie several times with a fork.

5. Place the ramekins on a baking sheet and bake in the preheated oven for about 20 minutes, until the pastry is puffed and golden brown. Leave to cool for about 10 minutes before serving.

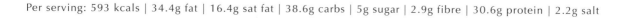

Per serving: 593 kcals | 34.4g fat | 16.4g sat fat | 38.6g carbs | 5g sugar | 2.9g fibre | 30.6g protein | 2.2g salt

CLAMS IN SPICY BROTH WITH CHORIZO

This festive, yet simple shellfish dish makes a lovely light meal served with a crisp green salad and fresh crusty bread to soak up the delicious broth.

SERVES 4   PREP: 25 MINUTES   COOK: 2 HOURS 25 MINUTES – 4 HOURS 25 MINUTES

1 tbsp olive oil

1 red onion, halved lengthways and sliced

115 g/4 oz chorizo sausage, diced

1 fennel bulb, coarsely chopped

400 g/14 oz canned chopped tomatoes, with juice

125 ml/4 fl oz dry white wine

125 ml/4 fl oz clam juice or water

½ tsp salt

¼ – ½ tsp crushed red pepper flakes

900 g/2 lb small clams, scrubbed

2 tbsp chopped fresh flat-leaf parsley, to garnish

125 g/4¼ oz green salad and 175 g/6 oz crusty bread, to serve

164

1. Heat the oil in a large frying pan over a medium–high heat. Add the onion and cook, stirring, for about 5 minutes, until soft. Add the chorizo and continue to cook, stirring occasionally, until the meat begins to brown. Transfer the mixture to the slow cooker.

2. Stir in the fennel, tomatoes and their can juices, wine, clam juice, salt and red pepper flakes. Cover and cook on high for about 2 hours or on low for about 4 hours.

3. Discard any clams with broken shells and any that refuse to close when tapped. Add the clams to the slow cooker, cover and cook on high for a further 10–15 minutes, until the clams have opened. Discard any clams that remain closed.

4. Serve the clams in bowls, with a generous amount of broth, garnished with parsley and accompanied by the green salad and crusty bread.

Per serving: 1564 kcals | 67.7g fat | 20.3g sat fat | 143.1g carbs | 31.1g sugar | 17.2g fibre | 73.7g protein | 11.6g salt

WILD MUSHROOM LASAGNE

You can use your slow cooker like a lasagne dish, layering up the ingredients and then leaving the slow cooker to its own devices.

SERVES 6   PREP: 35 MINUTES, PLUS SOAKING   COOK: 4 HOURS 35 MINUTES

15 ml/1 tbsp vegetable oil, for brushing
225 g/8 oz lasagne sheets
25 g/1 oz freshly grated Parmesan cheese

Filling
25 g/1 oz dried ceps
475 ml/16 fl oz boiling water
2 tbsp olive oil
1 small onion, diced
2 garlic cloves, finely chopped
450 g/1 lb button mushrooms or chestnut mushrooms, sliced
125 ml/4 fl oz red wine
1 tbsp finely chopped fresh thyme leaves
½ tsp salt
½ tsp pepper

Sauce
55 g/2 oz unsalted butter
35 g/1¼ oz plain flour
600 ml/1 pint milk
85 g/3 oz freshly grated Parmesan cheese
¾ tsp salt

1. To make the filling, soak the ceps in the water for 30 minutes. Remove the mushrooms, reserving the liquid, and chop. Heat the oil in a large frying pan over a medium–high heat. Add the onion and garlic and cook, stirring, for 5 minutes. Add the fresh and reconstituted mushrooms and cook, stirring, for about 5 minutes, until soft. Add the wine, bring to the boil and cook for about 5 minutes, until the liquid has almost evaporated. Add the mushroom soaking liquid, thyme, salt and pepper and cook over a medium–high heat, stirring frequently, for a further 5 minutes, or until the liquid is reduced by half.

2. To make the sauce, melt the butter in a large saucepan over a medium heat. Whisk in the flour and cook, whisking constantly, for about 3 minutes, until the mixture is golden brown. Whisk in the milk and bring to the boil. Reduce the heat and simmer for 3 minutes, then remove from the heat and stir in the cheese and salt.

3. To assemble the lasagne, line the slow cooker with foil, overlapping two large pieces to cover the entire base. Lightly brush the foil with oil. Spoon a thin layer of sauce and a thin layer of filling over the base. Top with a layer of pasta. Repeat twice, finishing with a final layer of pasta and then a layer of sauce. Top with a final layer of pasta, then a layer of sauce. Sprinkle the cheese over the top. Cover and cook on low for about 4 hours, until the pasta is tender and the top is brown and bubbling. Serve the lasagne directly from the slow cooker or use the foil as a sling to lift it out to serve.

Per serving: 476 kcals | 23.8g fat | 10.8g sat fat | 45.3g carbs | 8.1g sugar | 2.9g fibre | 18.1g protein | 2g salt

CRÈME BRÛLÉE

Everyone loves a crème brûlée, but not everyone has it as a regular dinner party pleaser – just sit back and enjoy the glory.

MAKES 6 PREP: 20 MINUTES, PLUS INFUSING, COOLING AND CHILLING COOK: 3 HOURS 5 MINUTES – 3 HOURS 35 MINUTES

1 vanilla pod
1 litre/1¾ pints double cream
6 egg yolks
100 g/3½ oz caster sugar
85 g/3 oz soft light brown sugar

1. Using a sharp knife, split the vanilla pod in half lengthways, scrape the seeds into a saucepan and add the pod. Pour in the cream and bring just to the boil, stirring constantly. Remove from the heat, cover and leave to infuse for 20 minutes.

2. Whisk together the egg yolks and caster sugar in a bowl until thoroughly mixed. Remove and discard the vanilla pod from the pan, then whisk the cream into the egg yolk mixture. Strain the mixture into a large jug.

3. Divide the mixture between 6 x 125-ml/4-fl oz ramekins and cover with foil. Stand the ramekins on a trivet in the slow cooker and pour in enough boiling water to come about halfway up the sides of the ramekins. Cover and cook on low for 3–3½ hours, until just set. Remove the slow cooker insert from the base and leave to cool completely, then remove the ramekins and chill in the refrigerator for at least 4 hours.

4. Preheat the grill to high. Sprinkle the brown sugar evenly over the surface of each dessert, then cook under the preheated grill for 30–60 seconds, until the sugar has melted and caramelized. Alternatively, you can use a cook's blowtorch. Return the ramekins to the refrigerator and chill for a further hour before serving.

168

Per serving: 474 kcals | 16.7g fat | 4.5g sat fat | 82.8g carbs | 59.3g sugar | 5.7g fibre | 4.3g protein | 0.2g salt

STRAWBERRY CHEESECAKE

This excellent cheesecake has a creamy strawberry filling – and who would have thought you could make this in a slow cooker?

SERVES 8   PREP: 20 MINUTES, PLUS COOLING   COOK: 2 HOURS 5 MINUTES, PLUS STANDING

85 g/3 oz unsalted butter, melted
140 g/5 oz digestive biscuits, crushed
300 g/10½ oz strawberries, hulled
600 g/1 lb 5 oz full fat soft cheese
225 g/8 oz caster sugar
2 large eggs, beaten
2 tbsp cornflour
finely grated rind and juice of 1 lemon

1. Stir the butter into the crushed biscuits and press into the base of a 20-cm/8-inch round springform tin, or a tin that fits into your slow cooker.

2. Purée or mash half the strawberries and whisk together with the cheese, sugar, eggs, cornflour, lemon rind and juice until smooth.

3. Tip the mixture into the tin and place in the slow cooker. Cover and cook on high for about 2 hours or until almost set.

4. Turn off the slow cooker and leave the cheesecake in the cooker for 2 hours. Remove and cool completely, then carefully turn out of the tin.

5. Decorate with the remaining sliced strawberries and serve.

171

Variation

YOU COULD REPLACE THE STRAWBERRIES WITH RASPBERRIES OR OTHER BERRIES, IF YOU PREFER.

Per serving: 491 kcals | 30.1g fat | 18.6g sat fat | 47.8g carbs | 36.1g sugar | 1.6g fibre | 7.7g protein | 0.8g salt

BUTTERSCOTCH PUDDINGS

These rich and creamy butterscotch puddings are divinely easy to make in the slow cooker.

MAKES 6   PREP: 20 MINUTES, PLUS COOLING AND CHILLING   COOK: 2 HOURS 5 MINUTES

2 tbsp unsalted butter

275 g/9¾ oz soft dark brown sugar

½ tsp salt

300 ml/10 fl oz double cream

175 ml/6 fl oz milk

4 egg yolks, lightly beaten

2 tsp vanilla extract

2 tsp whisky

30 ml/1 fl oz double cream, whipped, to serve

172

1. Fill the slow cooker with water to a depth of about 4 cm/ 1½ inches.

2. Melt the butter in a large saucepan over a medium heat. Add the sugar and salt and stir to mix well. Add the cream and milk and heat over a medium heat, until hot but not boiling.

3. Place the egg yolks in a medium-sized mixing bowl. Add the sugar and milk mixture in a very thin stream, whisking constantly. Whisk in the vanilla extract and whisky. Ladle the mixture into 6 x 125-ml/4-fl oz ramekins.

4. Carefully place the ramekins in the slow cooker, taking care not to slosh any of the water into them. Cover the slow cooker and cook on low for about 2 hours, or until the puddings are set.

5. Remove the ramekins from the slow cooker and transfer to a wire rack to cool for about 15 minutes, then cover with clingfilm, place in the refrigerator and chill for at least 2 hours before serving. Serve chilled, topped with a dollop of whipped cream.

Variation

IF YOU DON'T FANCY CREAM, VANILLA ICE CREAM IS ANOTHER WINNING SERVING SUGGESTION.

Per serving: 521 kcals | 33.9g fat | 20.4g sat fat | 48.5g carbs | 48g sugar | 0g fibre | 3.6g protein | 0.5g salt

INDEX